Our Minnesota

Photography and captions by Les and Craig Blacklock
Text by Fran Blacklock

Expanded Edition

VOYAGEUR PRESS

Photography and Captions by Les and Craig Blacklock

Text by Fran Blacklock

Editor: R. G. Murray

1st Printing
Copyright © 1978 by Les and Fran Blacklock

1st Revised Edition
Copyright © 1981 by Les and Craig Blacklock
All rights reserved
First published in 1978 by Voyageur Press
9337 Nesbitt Road, Bloomington, MN 55437
Library of Congress catalog card number: 78-70726
Typesetting, color lithography and binding by North Central Publishing Co., St. Paul
ISBN: 0-89658-006-7

NOTE FROM THE PUBLISHER

The 1973 Minnesota Seasons Calendar, the first Les Blacklock calendar, had a note from the editor as follows.

"Minnesota is most fortunate to have a man of Les Blacklock's ability and stature who feels a deep and sincere personal commitment to protecting our state. Choosing the photographs of Les' work was an enjoyable experience. My only problem was that I could only choose 13!

We decided that a calendar of Minnesota should emphasize the natural outdoors. All too often we hear complaints from people of other states about our cold winters, and Minnesotans have become defensive about it! But Minnesota is more than a state of cold winters — it is a state of "Four Seasons." These four seasons provide Minnesotans with diverse interests and activities.

Unfortunately, this calendar can give only a limited view of Minnesota. Hopefully Les will be able to add to it in subsequent years.

This is your calendar! We will welcome any comments to improve it."

The comments we received were ones of support and encouragement, including many requests for a permanent collection of photographs. In response to these requests, this book brings together your favorite photographs and vignettes from seven years of Minnesota Seasons. In addition, sixteen new photographs have been included.

Fran Blacklock, always in the background, has had unique opportunities to travel the state to learn its history and culture and appreciate its beauty. For that reason she was asked to share her impressions of the interesting, unusual and little known areas of Minnesota. This book is her personal journal depicting the highlights of 30 years of travelling the state with Les.

It is hoped that this sharing will encourage you to take back-road excursions and enjoy Our Minnesota as they have.

The publisher's note on the left was written when this book was first published in 1978. We received so many requests for a more permanent hardcover edition that we decided to not only make the book available in hardcover, but to expand it as well. The 32 additional full-color photographs which appear in this edition are among your favorites from the more recent Minnesota Seasons calendars.

Since the first edition was printed, Craig Blacklock has become a major contributor to the calendars, making the calendars and now this book truly a family affair.

All of us would like to thank you for your support in the past. We hope you like the additions made in this new edition of *Our Minnesota*.

The Publisher

Les and I have had an incurable love affair with Minnesota for many years now. While we were growing up, he in Moose Lake and I in Minneapolis, we took Minnesota more or less for granted. We were born here and there was no thought on our part or that of our parents of living anywhere else. As adults we have chosen to live in Minnesota.

This is a stimulating state to live in. Its variety spices things up considerably.

There is no "one look" to Minnesota. The southeastern corner fringed with the bluffs of the winding Mississippi River contrasts with the flat table-top fields of the northwestern section of the state. The northeastern Arrowhead region rimmed by the North Shore of Lake Superior with its evergreen forests and rock-shored lakes is rugged country, quite unlike the gentle lake lands of central Minnesota or the rolling farmlands of the southwest. Every region has character and interest of its own.

Our climate affords variety, too, making the "weather news" one of the most popular and necessary offerings on TV and radio.

In winter when the snow falls, it stays, accumulating for good skiing, snowshoeing, snowmobiling and other outdoor enjoyment. (Our highway department is equipped for and highly skilled at snow removal.) Snow simplifies the landscape. A covering of snow provides a new look to familiar scenes.

In late winter when the snow has melted and the streams are running free again, there are few fragrances as welcome as that moist freshness in the air that says, "spring!"

Each season in Minnesota has its own special sensation — something to anticipate. The return of songbirds and waterfowl in spring, the abundance of lush green growth and blue water in summer. The riot of color on trees and shrubs in autumn. The beauty of snowflakes and the graceful tracery of bare trees in winter. Without distinct seasons, the excitement of change wouldn't exist.

We enjoy the climate and the beauty of *Our Minnesota*.

Les and I had happy childhoods, and our environment was part of the reason. I lived near Lake Harriet where we kids hiked nearly every day in the summer to swim at the 48th Street beach. On Saturdays we often took a lunch and roamed along Minnehaha Creek or explored the marshes and pastureland around Diamond Lake. The Nicollet Avenue streetcar only went as far as 54th Street then, and it was country beyond that.

Les, living in the small town of Moose Lake, was closer to wild country. He recalls that as a boy he would often get up early and hike along the Moose Horn River before breakfast and school, watching the ducks and other wildlife, learning to read tracks and sharpening his powers of observation.

At the age of nine Les placed a can with cross hairs on a 98¢ box camera and took his first picture of ducks in flight. Seeing an image of the ducks, however blurred they were on the drugstore print, determined his future career. He was going to be a wildlife photographer.

One summer during his high school years he was a "savage" in Yellowstone Park, working as a clerk and soda jerk. But on his "off" hours he stalked big game with the family folding camera. He also gained outdoor experience through scouting and at YMCA Camp Miller at nearby Sturgeon Lake. Years of skiing through the woods and winter camping qualified him as an instructor in the Ski Troops in WW II.

Ironically, his regiment was disbanded and Les spent the last eighteen months of the war fighting in the jungles of the South Pacific with the Dixie Division.

Back home after the war, he still aimed at being a wildlife photographer, but there were no organized college courses leading to a W.P. degree. So on the GI Bill he designed his own course which he thought would be helpful to his career and took it at night school; photography, writing, speech, art, some informal wildlife courses and ceramics. That last course made the big difference in our lives. We met in that class.

We were married after a brief courtship.

NORTHEAST

On October 25, 1947, we set off on our honeymoon and my first canoe trip. I had assured everyone who doubted my sanity that if the weather was too bad we would change our plans, but inwardly I trusted my husband to take care of us no matter what.

My trousseau consisted of a pair of GI WAC shoes which cost $4 at a surplus store, a pair of wool pants, wool jacket, a wool ski bonnet and a pair of leather "chopper" mittens.

I left my wedding orchid at Gunflint Lodge on the Gunflint Trail in mid-afternoon on October 27, and climbed into the canoe which we had ordered as a wedding gift to ourselves. Justine Kerfoot and Janet Hanson, who were partners in a canoe outfitting business there, had named our canoe the "Voyageur," and on the bow seat had painted "To Fran from Les," and on the stern seat "To Les from Fran."

A few years later we painted the canoe red and it was the bright spot of color among the blues and greens of Les' pictures which Hamm's Beer used in its advertising "From The Land of Sky Blue Waters." The red canoe almost became a Hamm's trademark.

We told Janet and Justine the route we intended to follow and they said if we got snowed in they'd know where to send help.

With that reassurance we shoved off. Half way across Gunflint Lake I decided my seat needed the mittens more than my hands did. There wasn't enough insulation between me and the icy waters of the lake; I sat on my mittens and everything was fine.

Our honeymoon voyage followed the Canadian border route of lakes used by the French voyageurs from the early 1700's to the mid 1800's, now known as the Boundary Waters Canoe Area Wilderness.

We paddled and portaged through Gunflint and Magnetic Lakes, into the next small lake for our first campsite above Little Rock Falls. Huge clean rocks sloped down to the water's edge. Tall pines towered above us. Clear, sweet, drinkable water swept past us to tumble over the rocks into the next lake. We were in paradise.

Les got a small fire going so we could cook our first meal on the trail. It was to be bacon and eggs. I thought he was taking a long time rummaging in the food pack before he confessed — he had left the meat package back in his mother's refrigerator. But we did have eggs. Cooking utensils had somehow been left behind, too, but Les quickly whittled some out of a piece of wood and we still have them as souvenirs.

The mosquito season was long gone so we didn't need to put up a tent. It was before the days of air mattresses — at least we didn't have any — so Les prepared a springy base of reindeer moss for our sleeping bags. (We wouldn't do this today, but this was before there was heavy use of Canoe Country.)

As we lay that night looking up at the stars and full moon through the tree tops, we thought of the French voyageurs who had camped in this very spot long ago, carrying copper kettles and trade items to the West, bringing back furs for the fashionable people in Europe. And we thought of the explorers before them who had traveled the old Indian routes in search of the Northwest Passage to the Pacific Ocean and Asia in quest of spices.

These historic waterways remain almost unchanged by man in all the centuries he has traveled here.

The next day while Les was packing and loading the canoe, I lay down on a nice flat rock in the sun and promptly fell asleep. Les was considerate and fished below the falls and explored around camp while I slept and slept. I have found there's no mattress equal to a nice flat rock, if you're tired.

That day was not only sunny and warm, but still. Not a breath of air stirred. I had never experienced such absolute silence before as we glided along. Our silence was rewarded when we came upon a dark brown mink loping over the shoreline rocks, completely oblivious to our presence.

The second day ended with a glorious golden sunset to our left as we paddled down Pine Lake (now called Clove) at the same time a yellow moon was rising over the trees on our right. And straight ahead was a wedding cake island for our camp.

While I fixed dinner Les gathered balsam boughs for our bed. The fragrance of balsam in a springy bed of boughs, using just the tips of branches, can be the ultimate in sleeping comfort. (A bough bed is a "no-no" today because of increased use of campsites.)

The days were warm but the nights were below freezing. Each morning our sleeping bags, the trees, shrubs and grasses were all frosted. That's why I had brought along my ski bonnet — for a nightcap.

After another unbelievably calm day in which we moved from lake to lake through clean waters and deliciously balmy air without seeing another person, the sun set before we found a campsite. As we entered Round Lake (now called Gneiss), we scanned the shoreline and one rather light spot showed up. I learned that you can always make camp on a sand beach, and so we headed for it across the lake. As the canoe slid up on shore, Les jumped out exclaiming, "Moose, bear, wolf, deer tracks! Wow! Look at them." I was looking, but my excitement wasn't filled with joy. If I could have walked home at that moment, I would have, and it might have been a short marriage.

Les promised to keep a fire going by our sleeping bags if that would make me feel better. I imagined I saw glittering eyes peering at us from the darkness, but no four-footed intruders entered camp, and sleep soon overtook fear.

During our honeymoon I found a new love — canoe country. I wasn't being fickle. I had just added a wonderful new experience to my life. Familiar as I was with most of Minnesota, I had never entered this wilderness of waterways before. It is completely unlike any other part of our state. You are truly on your own, in a quiet, clean world of beauty.

Les and I have returned to explore new canoe routes many times since, and every time we are impressed by how precious, how fragile this wilderness is.

Minnesota State Bird — the Common Loon

When the American colonies were declaring independence from Britain, the long string of border lakes between Minnesota and Ontario had already seen nearly one hundred years of the white man's canoe traffic. Following routes long used by Indians, leather-moccasined Voyageurs carried furs that originated from as far away as the Lake Athabaska country in northwestern Canada. Today's *Voyageurs*, canoeists of all ages, still paddle and portage this unspoiled canoe country. The entire border route from the old North West fur post site on Rainy Lake, 250 miles east to the Grand Portage near Lake Superior, is *still* uncrossed by a road.

Before returning to Moose Lake where we were going to live, we roamed some of the back roads. The first night we spent in a deserted lumber camp off the Arrowhead Trail, inland from Hovland. It was owned by a friend, Vince Agurkis, who lived in Moose Lake. There was a huge pile of sawdust in the clearing. And since sawdust is good insulating material, Les had an idea. He dug into the pile a little ways and found it still had the warmth of August inside. So like two badgers, we burrowed into the sawdust until we had a cozy nest for ourselves and our sleeping bags.

And that wonderful aroma of warm sawdust! Few things stir the memory like fragrances, and the pungent smell of that sawdust transported me back to the age of eleven or twelve. My grandfather Eddy was a wholesale lumberman who took me with him one time to visit a lumber camp on the St. Croix River east of Rush City. I was fascinated, watching the men walking on the logs jammed in the river, pushing and pulling with their pike poles, guiding logs onto the "bullchain" that carried them into the mill. Inside the mill the screeching and squealing of the saw that sliced off boards first from one side of a log, then the other, was almost deafening. But, oh, that wonderful aroma of fresh sawn lumber! Almost equal to the smell coming from the mess hall where I was allowed to eat a sumptuous meal of beans, meat, potatoes, vegetables and pie with the men. No one ate heartier than the men in a lumber camp. This kind of camp belongs to an era that is all but passed, but the fragrant memory still lives.

Next morning in the deserted camp we were awakened by robin-sized gray birds calling to us. They were "camp robbers," "whiskey jacks," or, more properly named, gray jays, which frequent campsites where they can get a free meal. These were extremely tame birds and apparently very hungry, so much so that one hopped into the frying pan trying to steal a flapjack before we got it.

The next day of our northwoods honeymoon ended at the Cascade River on the North Shore of Lake Superior. There was an undeveloped opening in the woods then and at that season we had it to ourselves for a camp. The Cascade was to be the setting for an adventure that winter. The river tumbles in a series of narrow waterfalls through a rock-walled gorge before it flows into Lake Superior just below the North Shore Drive bridge. Good trails follow the river and a foot bridge crossing the canyon is used by deer as well as people. The lakeshore near the river is one of our favorite places in a high wind when the waves are crashing on the jagged rocks. The rhythm of the ca-whumping and the after-splash are almost hypnotic and I could spend hours happily hypnotized by the surf, watching gulls soaring and dipping overhead.

When the sun dropped behind the inland hills, we had to consider what we were going to use for our mattress that night. It turned out to be hay which we harvested from the abundant grasses in the clearing.

The finale of our honeymoon was a concession to our bond with

The traditional reds and greens of Christmas are about as intense as they can be on the northwoods forest floor. Bunchberries, here with the Christmas-fragrant balsam, remind me of grade school wreaths made with construction paper or colored with crayons. We wanted the *reddest* red and *greenest* green we could find.

High Falls — Baptism River

civilization. We exchanged camp clothes for our wedding suits and drove to Duluth for lunch at the Flame (now Anchor Inn). It still affords a good view of the ore boats and steamers from all over the world passing under the famous Aerial Bridge into the harbor of Duluth.

One of the most striking examples of early buildings preserved for the future is the old Duluth Union Depot, now the St. Louis County Heritage and Arts Center. The chateau-like structure, built in 1892, has massive fireplaces and interesting detail. Exhibits include many historic trains used in early Minnesota and memorabilia of logging days.

Duluth is one of the most interesting cities in Minnesota, insanely but excitingly built on the steep rocky hills above Lake Superior. Its strategic geographical location at the head of the Great Lakes has made it a leading port for shipping iron ore and agricultural and manufactured products to cities in the East and foreign countries. Huge grain elevators and gigantic ships being loaded with grain and ore make a sight-seeing cruise of the harbor a tourist delight. Another tourist "must" is Skyline Parkway which winds its way along the top of the hill connecting Duluth's parks and campuses, leading to Hawk Ridge Nature Reserve at the east end, the best place in the nation to watch migrating hawks in autumn. The hawks follow the shoreline on their way south, soaring with the air currents. At Hawk Ridge they often flare up just a few feet above the heads of watchers. Weather conditions cause variations in flight

If the character of a body of water is determined by its *shores* (any large lake or sea looks much like any other except for its shores), then Lake Superior must rank very high among Earth's beautiful waters. Minnesota's North Shore of Lake Superior is cooled in summer, warmed in winter by the great lake. Explored by voyageurs, studied by geologists, home of trappers, loggers and fishermen, the North Shore is still wild, rugged and unspoiled along much of its length.

patterns, but as many as 71,000 raptors have been sighted in one fall count.

Duluth is probably the best place in Minnesota to see many other birds too. Minnesota Point, a sandy bar across the mouth of the St. Louis River starting at the Aerial Bridge, is a "migrant trap" for thousands of birds in spring and fall. Loons, grebes, ducks, gulls, and shorebirds can be seen there.

On the third of November, 1947, it was still autumn, even though there was a definite chill in the air. But on November 5, two days after our canoe trip, there were fourteen inches of snow on the ground that stayed all winter, soon topped by many more inches of the white fluff.

Right after Christmas we started organizing for Les' long-anticipated adventure. He was going to live with the deer herd that wintered along the North Shore in one of the largest concentrations near the Cascade River. The climate near the shore is tempered by the lake and south exposure, and the snow is usually not as deep as it is inland, so this is where the deer "yard up" in the winter.

As their numbers increase they consume more and more of the vegetation that sustains them. When their numbers grow too great, they begin to run out of food. They will have eaten cedar branches (their favorite food) as high as they can reach and the tips of mountain maple and red osier dogwood until they finally kill the bushes. Then starvation is a threat. Les intended to record how the deer at the Cascade "yard" fared during the winter to put it in a book to be called "Deer Diary."

Harry Jones, a co-worker of mine at the Star and Tribune before my marriage, convinced Les to take a movie camera, too. So our savings went into the purchase of a 16 mm motion picture camera and food supplies. We made up many pounds of hamburger patties and froze them, and packed many kinds of food that wouldn't be harmed by freezing.

We loaded the car with food and camping gear and drove up the North Shore of Lake Superior one shining winter day the first of February. Lake Superior can be frozen one day and open the next depending upon the wind. Very seldom is it all frozen over. This day it was sparkling blue with white gulls soaring on the air currents and noisy old squaw ducks zipping above the waves.

In winter it's possible to see much further into the woods than in summer, when leaves on trees and bushes screen your vision. Beyond the city of Two Harbors, we began to see deer and every one of them was a thrill. Some were leaping away from the road with their tails waving like white flags. Others would watch us, ears alert, while some were undisturbed and pursued their business of finding tender tips of shrubs to nibble, or were standing on their hind legs to reach for branches. If a substantial part of a deer's diet is

Most of the shoreline of Lake Superior, the largest body of fresh water in the world, is still natural. Although there is almost constant movement of the water, varying from a light swish to the pounding of mountainous breakers, the basic shape of the pre-Cambrian rock shore has changed very, very slowly.

Frosted Norway Pine and Oak

This fat fawn knows what's good for her! She's been nosing around in the soft snow for acorns. Thriving on her mother's milk, then being weaned to a large assortment of succulent plants and shrubs all summer and fall, and nipping twigs and digging for acorns during the winter, she has multiplied her weight at least ten times from her four to five pounds at birth. She isn't quite as fat as she looks, because her thin, red, white-spotted summer coat has been replaced with a two-inch blanket of hollow-haired insulation. Even so, she's a dandy nine-month-old deer, doing very well, thank you!

balsam, it means the deer may be close to starvation. Balsam fills their stomachs, but doesn't provide sufficient nutrition for deer.

It was evident by the number of deer we were seeing that many had moved to the shore from inland forests to yard up for the remainder of the winter. (On one trip we counted well over 200 deer from the car, between Duluth and Grand Marais.)

At the Cascade River we parked and unloaded the supplies that were to keep Les fed, warm and equipped to photograph deer for the next two months — snowshoes, a single burner gasoline stove, a mummy-type sleeping bag, mukluks and other boots, parkas and on and on. I drove back to Moose Lake leaving Les to carry his gear to a protected opening far up in the woods.

On March 15 I returned by Greyhound bus that dropped me off at the Cascade River. I was to photograph Les showing how he lived in camp and worked with the deer, to fit into the motion picture he was making. We thought this was a good time of year to do this; the sun was higher and days were growing longer and warmer.

Les hadn't set up our small GI mountain tent until my arrival. He had been sleeping under the stars on a bough bed on top of the deep snow. But as a concession to me he put up the tent and built a fire for the first time. He believes that it's best not to depend on a fire for warmth, otherwise you won't want to leave it. So he dressed for the extreme cold and fared very well.

I had borrowed a parka and every piece of cold weather clothing I could lay my hands on and I was ready for a week in the woods.

Les' thermometer registered fifteen degrees above zero the afternoon I arrived — a nice balmy winter temperature. But the next morning the mercury was barely visible at 33 degrees below zero!

Les learned in the ski troops that the best way to keep warm in a sleeping bag is without any clothing on. Socks and clothes are kept warm and dry by placing them between the inner and outer bags while you sleep. But there comes a time when one must bare one's body to the outer air in order to get dressed (or undressed) and the thin skin of our unheated tent didn't do much to keep out the cold.

Les got a fire going while I reluctantly forced myself to get out of the bag and dressed. At least in the deep woods the frigid northwest wind was slowed down considerably. Once out of the tent, clutching a steaming cup of coffee with mittened hands, I found myself edging up closer and closer to the fire until I was almost in it, trying to absorb some of its warmth. I could see the fire and smoke but I couldn't feel much heat. And somehow my usually cheery voice fell silent. As the sun rose higher but the temperature didn't, my spirits "froze" along with my feet. In spite of constantly pacing or walking, my feet were cold and my boots, which were wrong for this kind of outing, froze with turned up toes. *I was miserable!*

But thankfully, Cascade Lodge, on the North Shore about a half mile from camp, was able to accommodate us at night until the deep freeze ended three days later. My voice returned and my spirits rose with the temperature. We snowshoed to the areas Les had worked with the deer, and I had fun being a cinematographer.

Beyond the unbelievability of gazing at open water when the mercury has dropped well below zero is the sheer beauty of it. White curtains of mist rise and twist loose from the warm womb that bore them. The dance is a mesmerizing one. As I watch the ice, the water and fog playing their liquid round, all the lives and rivers and seas that this water has passed through seem to be flowing with it — the past bound to the future by a common drop of water. — C.B.

Evening Grosbeak

Split Rock Lighthouse, on Minnesota's North Shore of Lake Superior, is not the classic round, white spire often pictured on rocky coasts, but the old guardian *is* picturesque, high on its sheer cliff, preserved for its historic value as well as its handsomeness. The lighthouse and land around it are now a state park, and as you might suspect of so romantic a subject, very popular.

(When the film was completed, Les used it as a lecture film called, "I Lived With the Deer," for about two years. Later it was condensed to a ten-minute version with sound track, re-titled "Deer Live With Danger," distributed by Encyclopaedia Britannica Films.)

The following summer we went back to the North Shore and Grand Marais, one of our favorite Minnesota towns. Encouraged by a visual education faculty member at the University of Minnesota who had seen Les' deer footage, we borrowed $1,000 to purchase a better movie camera and other equipment to film the moose of Isle Royale National Park in Lake Superior. Our take-off point was Grand Marais, and at 3:00 a.m. on July 5 we were awakened by the skipper of the Detroit who found us where we were sleeping on the outer rocks of the harbor. The Detroit was a tub-bottomed riverboat owned by a Duluth fish company. It had been converted for use on the high seas of Lake Superior to pick up fish from the commercial fishermen who lived from spring through fall along the picturesque rocky fjords of the island. It also took them supplies and once in a while carried passengers. We camped and photographed on Isle Royale four-and-a-half months before returning to Minnesota.

The Detroit no longer exists but the service to the fishermen goes on, and boats, which also carry passengers, start from Grand Portage National Monument farther up the shore.

Grand Portage is worth a visit all by itself. As the name implies, this was the beginning of a long portage for the French voyageurs. They carried their trade goods or furs overland for nine miles to avoid the rapids and falls of the Pigeon River which form the border between Canada and the United States at this point. The trail, used by Indians long before the white men arrived, starts at a gap in the continuous hills on the lake shoreline.

Here on a protected bay of Lake Superior was the first white settlement in Minnesota. Inland exploration searching for a route to the Pacific, the sea of the west, had started here as long ago as 1679 when Sieur DuLhut explored the region. The city of Duluth is named for him. Fort St. Charles was established on Lake of the Woods in 1732 by La Verendrye, another early explorer. Many traders and explorers traveled the border canoe routes in the years after that, setting up innumerable trading posts. But it wasn't until 1768 that the site of Grand Portage village was cleared and a fort built.

Every year canoes loaded with furs would arrive from inland wintering posts for the annual meeting at Grand Portage. Furs would be exchanged for supplies and trade goods which had been brought by large Montreal freighter canoes through the Great Lakes. One can imagine also the exchange of stories — tragedies of lives lost in capsized canoes, illness (hernia was common), violence, whether from nature or man, and rollicking tales of good humor. And songs, for voyageurs sang from morning to night on the trail and were often

As I look down on the Great Hall of Grand Portage National Monument from up here on Mt. Rose, after a warming climb on snowshoes, I wonder how different the scene would have been when this was a fur trade center. The old fur post here on the north shore of Lake Superior is being reconstructed as it was in the 18th and early 19th centuries. Sixteen more buildings within the stockade will match as closely as possible the original busy center.

Grand Portage was the meeting place of large freight canoes from the east and the tough little *voyageurs* who paddled and portaged furs here from a tremendous area north and west. The nine mile Grand Portage Trail, bypassing waterfalls on the Pigeon River, tied Grand Portage to literally thousands of miles of wilderness canoe trails.

Palisade Head.

Clinging tenaciously to rocks and life, Grand Portage, Minnesota's ancient Witch Tree makes me wonder. Its roots take sustenance from little more than the leaves it drops, yet it may outlive many a younger tree growing in rich soil in the forest. Is all of life like that? Would *humans* be tougher, stronger, better able to survive the storms ahead if we used *less* of the world's resources?

hired for their singing ability. And drinking, for this must have been a time for celebration and revelry.

Once their business was transacted, the fur trading voyageurs returned to their inland wintering posts until the next year.

This was long before the days of government surveys and detailed maps of the labyrinth of waterways. But these men devised an interesting means of marking their routes through the lakes. A voyageur was chosen to climb a tall pine along the route. With an ax he would chop or lob off the middle branches, leaving a great plume as a visible marker that could be seen from a long distance. Some of these voyageur lob pines have survived well into this century. But a recent lob pine, cut by Boy Scouts on Crane Lake, honors Sigurd F. Olson whose efforts are greatly responsible for the preservation of the border route wilderness.

The Grand Portage Fort has been rebuilt twice in recent times, (the first restoration was hit by lightning and burned to the ground), faithfully following the original plans, even to the color of the paint.

Les and I have paddled out into the harbor and tried to imagine how it would have seemed to approach the Fort after the long gruelling and often treacherous trip through the Great Lakes from Montreal. Even though the paddlers tried to hug shorelines, there were times they had to cross wide stretches of open water where sudden storms could overtake them. The sight of Grand Portage at the end of their voyage must have been very welcome.

Inside the restored Great Hall we have seen an excellent film depicting the rigorous life of the voyageur.

A trail leads up Mt. Rose behind the Fort for a panoramic view of Lake Superior. Twenty-two miles from shore, Isle Royale sometimes appears to float on the distant horizon. You can also hike all or part of the Grand Portage trail as we have, and try to imagine carrying two 90-pound packs on your back. That was standard (some carried more) for the sturdy little Frenchmen who were among the first white men to venture this far west.

From Grand Portage it's a short and scenic drive to the border and into Canada to the High Falls of the Pigeon River. This magnificent cataract thunders into a deep rocky gorge. Our young son coined the word "fantalastical!" to describe it. The falls is on the U.S. Canadian border. If it were all in Minnesota, it would be the highest falls in the state.

Traveling along the shore of Superior only part of the beauty can be appreciated from a car. We like to park the car and hike the trails that follow the streams and rivers flowing into the lake. Most of them have lovely waterfalls, each one different. A mountainous road goes to the top of Palisade Head for a breathtaking view from the sheer rock cliff above the blue-green water. We have found blueberries growing among the rocks on the hill early in August. In fact, blueberry patches occur all through northeastern Minnesota.

Shovel Point, visible to the east from Palisade Head, has trails to

What's around the next bend, the next and the next . . . that's what canoe-tripping is. It's exploring country that has changed very little since the forest returned after the last great ice sheet melted.

The world's finest canoe country, two hundred miles of shared wilderness between Minnesota and Ontario, is headwaters. Over the bulk of it there is only wilderness upstream, so the island-studded lakes and waterways are drinkable. That is a rare and beautiful situation, almost unique in the world.

the tip of the point where the waves dash dramatically on windy days. From the point there is a good view of the Sawtooth Mountain Range, whose formation resembles the jagged teeth of a saw.

Split Rock Lighthouse makes an interesting stop. No longer needed as a navigation aid, the light and the surrounding land have been preserved as a state park. The trail up Day's Hill from the Wayside Stop gives a good view of the lighthouse.

Along the Shore some of the most scenic and unique areas have been protected and preserved in state parks. George H. Crosby-Manitou State Park is different from the others. Park headquarters and the take-off point for trails are inland, eight miles northeast of Finland, a town on Highway 1. The park has nine miles of backpacking trails with many small primitive campsites in a mountainous rock and forest area. The main trail ends at Highway 61 on the North Shore. We have hiked upstream from the highway after photographing spectacular Manitou Falls.

The Arrowhead, Gunflint, Caribou and Sawbill Trails penetrate inland from the shore to a forested land of lakes, streams, wildlife and places to explore.

One summer we worked on the lakes along these trails making the Minnesota portion of a fishing film called, "Cast of Three." (The other two portions were filmed in Wyoming and North Carolina.) We sought photogenic sites and good fishing waters in all three states. In Minnesota's Arrowhead region the possible locations were almost limitless and working conditions close to sublime.

Some of our favorite wilderness roads are Highway 1, inland from Illgen City, County Road 2 north from Two Harbors, both leading to Ely and its magnificent lake country, and the Echo Trail northwest from Ely to Crane Lake. A quick look at the state map shows how few roads penetrate the borderland wilderness. Once you leave the roads the land and lakes are much the same as when the voyageurs traveled by birchbark canoes. Today we can still go by canoe, snowshoe or skis, and in certain areas, by motorboat and snowmobile.

Farther west along the border is the new Voyageur National Park, still under development. This is a water-oriented park including Rainy, Kabetogama and Namakan Lakes, large and beautiful border lakes traveled by the voyageurs, and the Kabetogama Peninsula. There will be no roads on the peninsula, accessible only by boat or canoe.

If ancient pines in Voyageurs National Park could speak, they would have colorful tales to tell. They were here when the voyageurs came paddling by, singing their French cadence songs.

West of Voyageurs National Park, International Falls is a bustling city whose paper mill uses what looks like endless stockpiles of logs.

Shortly after the turn of the century my father signed up for a homestead on the West Fork of the Black River and took the train to International Falls from Minneapolis. From the Falls he traveled down the Rainy River by steamer to Loman, a single house that served as postoffice. From Loman he had to walk nine miles to his claim at the end of the trail. He was a young city-bred minister's son with no knowledge of the northwoods or cabin building.

As a child I never tired of hearing about how his neighbors on the trail helped him build his cabin and barn before winter set in, how his winter's supply of potatoes and vegetables froze when his woodstove went out, and other experiences of northwoods survival.

The first night he spent in the cabin he thought he heard shooting outside, only to learn later that it was beavers slapping their tails in the water. Isolation was new to him, and he soon grew so lonesome he sent for the family dog. But the dog was lonesome, too, and his endless howling only made matters worse. Dad finally shipped him back to Minneapolis.

After six months the claim was legally his. He "proved up," went back to Minneapolis, married my mother and settled down to an urban life, his taste for adventure apparently satisfied.

When I was in high school our family took a camping trip through northern Minnesota. We went to Loman, and the same couple were running the postoffice in their home. They remembered Dad. We wanted to hike in and see if his cabin was still there. They told us all the claims had been deserted and the trail grown over so we couldn't get through. Although I have seen many tumbling-down homestead cabins in northern Minnesota, relics of shattered dreams and hard work, I still have a hankering to see Dad's place. Maybe someday.

To the west and south of Loman is a lot of blank space on the state map. This is the Big Bog, where muskeg, scattered spruce, cedar and tundra-like vegetation stretch farther than the eye can see.

Abandoned farms have a beauty about them which only time can produce; the aging of the buildings, the variety of new growth as cultivated land and pasture slowly evolve to prairie, then shrubland, and finally back to forest. And during the hundred years or so this all takes, the farm is as rich in wildlife as this land will ever be.

Winterberry (Minnesota) Holly

As the last glint of gold leaves the snow, and the silhouetted spruce blend into the dark of night, I must leave this northwoods bog. My fingers have grown numb fumbling with the frozen metal of my camera, and my eyes cannot penetrate the darkness. I am out of my natural environment and in that of the bog creatures. Soon in this winter fairyland, tales will be written in the snow . . . of ruffed grouse diving into insulating fluff to spend the night, ready to explode from their shelter if danger threatens; snowshoe hares hopping about beneath the protective spruce, pursued by coyotes or possibly timber wolves; mice scurrying about in their tunnels, and a red fox trotting nose down in search of them, hoping that each leap into the air will land on dinner, taking several tries to secure at least a one-mouse supper . . . a whole series of life and death adventures, clearly told by the tracks to be read the following morning. — C.B.

Minnesota State Tree — the Red (Norway) Pine

My first year after graduation from the University, I taught in Baudette on the Rainy River. Driving through mile after mile of the Bog to get there, I felt I was going to the end of the world. I have since learned to appreciate the abundance of life that lives in bogs and so I could look at it quite differently today. But it still is *awfully* big.

From Baudette where I had a great year learning to know a very wild part of our state and a lot of fine folks, there is easy access to beautiful Lake of the Woods, a favorite of fishermen, from either the American or Canadian sides.

Until recently there was no road to that isolated piece of Minnesota called the Northwest Angle that sticks up like a thumb at the top of the state map. Through a quirk in establishing the U.S.-Canadian boundary back in 1783, this small piece of Minnesota is surrounded by Canada and Lake of the Woods. Most of the few people living on the Angle have liked their isolation, when access was mostly by boat or seaplane, but now there is a road approach through Canada from Warroad.

Ft. St. Charles, the fort and fur trading post of La Verendrye in the early 1700's, has been restored. It is on Magnuson's Island just off the Angle shoreline.

Rainbows are usually associated with summer thunderstorms, but a waterfall mistbow happens every sunny day. Here is the unusual combination of fall color and the magic that happens when sunlight hits air borne drops of water.

Fireweed

With breath-taking views in several directions, the climb to the top of the Palisades on Seagull Lake is well worth the effort. And in season the blueberries on top are a dandy bonus! The grand, rugged scenery, the wildness, the cleanness, the rare, unspoiled virgin forest — all document the wisdom of preserving the Boundary Waters Canoe Area. This quiet wilderness can help a visitor get to know himself and his relationship to his world.

Southwest from Ely are the great Iron ranges of Minnesota — the Vermilion, Mesabi and Cuyuna. At Tower-Soudan, the deep underground mine was closed in 1962 when the rich ore deposits ran out. The mine and over a thousand acres were donated as a state park. The elevator ride down 2400 feet followed by a three-mile train ride through a mining tunnel is a unique experience in Minnesota. We were fascinated just watching the man skillfully manipulating the controls that run the elevator. He and many of the guides were former miners.

The largest mines are open pit mines, because iron-bearing strata occurs near the surface. Looking over these vast pits is something akin to a view of the Grand Canyon. The world's largest open pit iron mine can be seen from the Hull-Rust Viewpoint located near Hibbing. The view over the Rouchleau Mine at Virginia, called Viewpoint in the Sky, is from a 20-story stockpile. The gigantic equipment used to dig and haul ore look like toys from a distance, but at close range they are monsters. Information Centers are located at many points throughout the Range cities to guide visitors.

An Iron Range Interpretative Center is south of Chisholm on Highway 169 on the brink of the old Pillsbury mine. With creative and space-age techniques, visitors get a meaningful grasp of iron mining and taconite production from all aspects. The Minnesota Museum of Mining located at Chisholm is well worth a visit, too, with a simulated trip through a mine and the chance to climb up on huge mining equipment.

The funsters were here! River otters, the animal clowns, have left a story in the snow. Those water imps may be back tomorrow, next week, next month, or never again, depending on how good the fishing is, if there's a steep sliding hill nearby, or pure whim. If *I* were an otter, I'd sure be tempted to stay awhile at this lovely opening on the Sea Gull River near the Canadian border.

A few years ago Les and I had an assignment to cover the entire state of Minnesota, recording in words and pictures the many things of interest there are to see and do. Our work was published in booklets featuring six regions of the state, the first in a number of series published by the Department of Business Development.

It was a wonderful experience for us to learn to know Minnesota and her people in every nook and cranny of the state. From sunup until after dark each day, we journeyed from town to town travelling more than 7,000 miles, talking with people, and learning about places of scenic beauty or special interest.

Along with feasting our eyes on the scenery, we marvelled at the people. In visiting hundreds of tourist attractions, shops, museums, resorts, we never met any who were not genuinely interested in telling us about their places, many of them the result of a personal hobby such as collecting, or skills such as wood carving, taxidermy and potting.

Curving gracefully through Christmas card scenery, the Gunflint Trail penetrates the northwoods wilderness from Grand Marais on the north shore of Lake Superior. Surrounded by the unique Boundary Waters Canoe Area Wilderness, a person at the far end of the Trail is nearly forty miles from the next road to the north. Straight north there are but three roads between this point and the North Pole!

Little Rock Falls — Boundary Waters Canoe Area Wilderness

He's called *brush wolf* in the north woods, but he's really a coyote, and he ranges far beyond his traditional prairie home. Welcomed by cattle raisers for controlling rodents, hated by sheep ranchers, the controversial little wolf has gotten lots of folks mad at each other. Persistent poison 1080 (now banned) aimed at the coyote, killed thousands of non-target animals and birds such as the golden eagle. And that *really* got folks upset! In spite of intensive trapping and poisoning, the coyote has thrived and now roams over most of North America.

Hiawatha and Minnehaha

TWIN CITIES AREA

The Twin Cities of Minneapolis and St. Paul have many things to be proud of — theatre, music, sports, restaurants, museums and galleries, colleges and universities, the state capitol complex, downtown business districts that have received face lifts — and we have enjoyed and benefited from them all. Pick up any newspaper and there are dozens of choices of things to do advertised on its pages.

But one of the things that doesn't often get top billing is what makes the Cities very special — their wealth of scenic green spaces.

The winding Mississippi River threads its way through the very heart of the cities. One summer my brother worked on the tugboat Demopolis that pushed strings of barges between St. Paul and Minneapolis. He commented on how, once he left the city centers, it was like boating through wild land, the river banks are so steep and forested. Excursion boats now make the same delightful trip and historic points are mentioned along the way.

Parkways connect chains of lakes, golf courses, beautiful spacious parks, and follow Minnehaha Creek to the Falls made famous by Longfellow. A trail at the base of the Falls follows the Creek through a glen to the Mississippi River.

Henry Wadsworth Longfellow gave world renown to Minnehaha Falls in his poem, "The Song of Hiawatha." But this lovely cascade would have been well known without Hiawatha; after all, Longfellow knew of its beauty only from reading about it in his library in Massachusetts! Even though surrounded by the cities of Minneapolis and St. Paul, Minnehaha Falls performs in an idyllic setting, and the creek winds through a wild valley below the falls to its confluence with the Mississippi River. I photographed the scene with a 4 × 5 Speed Graphic camera. Ektachrome film, exposed for 1/25 second, to approximate the blur of the falls as it appears to the eye.

Fort Snelling

Fort Snelling State Historical Park is just "a stone's throw" from busy Metropolitan Airport, off Highway 55. A visit to the Fort, first completed in 1825 but only recently reconstructed, provides a vivid trip back in time to how life was lived in the early days of the Fort. It definitely wasn't fancy. Guides dressed as soldiers, or soldiers' wives, of the 1820's speak and act every bit as if they were living in the early Fort. During a recent visit the Fort residents told us about life on this isolated, rugged frontier as we were seated on benches in the one-room schoolhouse. We climbed to the top of the famous round tower with its super-thick walls and well-placed gun holes. The baker was building a wood fire inside a brick oven and told us how many dozens of the hard round loaves of bread he baked each day for the soldiers' rations. The blacksmith was hammering out a candle stand for the colonel's house. The woodworker was turning a chair leg with an ingenious homemade device, using a willow branch cut along the riverbank. The sutler sold us some spruce gum which was considered a treat in those days.

While appreciating the cool shade of this silver maple in Fort Snelling State Park, I formed a frame with my hands and decided that there was a scene here worth photographing, of this quiet backwater of the Minnesota River. — L.B.

For many years Fort Snelling was the only spot of civilization in this vast area. Here, more than any other place, was the beginning of Minnesota as we know it.

The entrance to the lower level of the state park is from Highway 5 at the Post Road. There are places for swimming, boating, canoeing, fishing, hiking, snowmobiling and skiing. The park includes Pike Island which can be seen from the Mendota Bridge at the confluence of the Mississippi and Minnesota Rivers. Lt. Zebulon Pike (of Pike's Peak fame) met here with the Dakota (Sioux) in 1805 to purchase land for the Fort for $200 worth of rum, some gifts and a promise of $2,000 more. Today there is a nature center on the island.

A companion piece to Ft. Snelling in Minnesota's early history, is the **Sibley House** just across the Mendota Bridge. A tour of this substantial stone house, built in 1835 by Henry Sibley, Minnesota's first governor, and the Faribault House, built by his neighbor and fur trader, Jean Faribault, now a museum of rare Indian crafts, can fill a fascinating afternoon. St. Peter's Church, up the hill, is the oldest church in the state.

The Minnesota River Valley, for many miles upstream from Ft. Snelling State Park, has been authorized by Congress to be a Federal Wildlife Refuge and Wildlife Recreation Area. A trail system will follow the river. At the time of Congress' authorization, Senator Hubert Humphrey said the area would "broaden man's

Mendota Bridge

My stomach urged me to stop waiting for just the right light and *eat supper*. But the late-setting summer sun was starting to cast purple tree-shadows across the sturdy face of the Sibley House, so I waited. The oldest permanent residence in Minnesota was built in 1835 by the man who was to become the state's first governor, Henry H. Sibley. Because of the late hour, I had this bit of history all to myself. It's easier to imagine the buck-skinned and top-hatted visitors of that period without modern cars and crowds of camera-flashers around.

Lotus in Bloom

The *Josiah Snelling* and its mate, the *Jonathan Padelford*, cruise the Mississippi through a flood-plain wilderness right in the heart of the Minneapolis-St. Paul metro area. Deer, fox, raccoon, beaver and many other species of wildlife frequent the winding shores within a few hundred yards of busy highways and business complexes.

understanding and appreciation of the environment,'' providing opportunities for hiking, bird watching, photography, nature study, hunting, fishing and other activities. "We now have the means,'' he said, ''to assure that the pressure of urban development will not deny future generations the opportunity to enjoy this irreplaceable natural asset.''

The Minnesota River Valley Restoration Project is just east of Shakopee at Murphy's Landing on the Minnesota River. It grows more interesting as it develops each year. The old Pond Grist Mill sparked the whole idea. Fallen into disrepair, the Shakopee Fire Department was going to burn it several years ago in a fire-fighting exercise. But before they got around to it, a local contractor who felt the building should be preserved, put on a new roof and boarded up the windows, making it too valuable to burn.

Margaret Mac Farlane, an art teacher in the Shakopee High School, became interested in the possibility of restoring the mill. She obtained a leave of absence to work on it and the whole restoration idea has grown from the mill that *didn't get burned*.

The Minnesota Valley Restoration Project is a living museum of Dakota (Sioux) Indian lodges, old log cabins, stores, a depot and significant farms and homes that have been moved to this site and placed chronologically so visitors can walk from one decade to the next, from 1840 to the turn of the century. A large Indian village once existed here and there are Indian mounds on the site dating

Early Farm — Minnesota Valley Restoration Project

Placed among the soft mounds of a northern hardwood forest, this small lake says "somewhere in central Minnesota.''
Non-Minnesotans might scoff in disbelief if you told them that the lake is in Minneapolis, but Minnesotans know that Minneapolis is the City of Lakes, so they wouldn't question it. Minneapolis it is, in Theodore Wirth Park.

Burwell House — Minnetonka Mills

June, warm and moist, is the month of growth. Vegetation is at its greenest and fair weather clouds float by one beautiful day after another. Minneapolitans own this world of green and blue that encompasses their priceless chain of lakes. — L.B.

from 300 B.C. to the 18th century. Typical bark lodges and skin tipis have been recreated at the start of the walk through time. The Oliver Faribault fur trading cabin is the first pioneer home, followed by an 1850 and then an 1880 farm with livestock, ending with a typical river village of 1890 and the Pond Grist Mill at its original location. From May to September, "residents" of the homes and "shopkeepers" demonstrate actual lifestyles of the period. A river nature trail adds another facet to this visit to the 19th Century.

The newest "must" on the list of interesting things to do around the Twin Cities is the **Minnesota Zoo**, which opened in May, 1978. Termed a "major world zoological attraction," it has used every concept possible for visitors to see animals and birds in natural-looking habitats, rather than in cages. Imagine touching noses underwater with cavorting white whales (except for the dividing glass wall). It is possible to watch beavers build dams, and approximately 400 other species of the animal kingdom "doing their thing" amid the lakes and rolling wooded hills of the 480-acre park. Some of the more unusual inhabitants are Japanese snow monkeys, Siberian tigers, musk oxen, Asiatic horses, Bactrian camels and moose. Animals can be petted and fed in the Children's Zoo. The Zoo is located south of the Minnesota River, east of I-35W on Johnny Cake Ridge Road.

For those who love wildflowers — and who doesn't — the **Eloise Butler Wildflower Garden** in Theodore Wirth Park above Birch Pond in Minneapolis is the place to go, especially in spring and summer when the flowers are in bloom. Most of the wild flowers native to Minnesota grow here in wild settings of wooded glens, marsh and prairie — a bit of quiet wilderness in the city.

Unlike many areas or buildings named for wealthy benefactors, the Eloise Butler Wildflower Garden was named for a retired botany teacher. After working without compensation to tend and preserve this wild wooded land, along with other botany teachers, Miss Butler was made its first official curator in 1911 at a very modest salary. In 1929 the "Natural Botanical Garden" was renamed for her, and she continued to give the plants and birds loving care until her death in the garden in 1933 at the age of 81.

One of our favorite visits any time of year has been to the **Minnesota Landscape Arboretum**, west of the cities on Highway 5. The many varieties of trees, shrubs and plants that grow in Minnesota are here in beautifully landscaped beds, or in wild prairie, woodland or marshy pockets. A roadway winds through this extensive area, but to really appreciate what is there, the footpaths from parking areas are a better way to go. The impressive French chateau headquarters has an excellent nature library whose unusual tables are worth a visit by anyone who appreciates fine wood. The dining room is a delightful place to enjoy lunch by the fireplace or on the patio.

Our largest northern orchid, the Showy Lady's-Slipper, is endangered wherever there are people. I have heard of many places where they *used* to be abundant, but have never seen a large wild stand. I am torn between wanting to share the delicate beauty of this Minnesota state flower, and not telling anyone where they are.

In order to be a wildlife photographer, Les has had to know the habits of the animals and birds, where to find them, their diets, their relationship to other wildlife and their environment. It was a rather logical development that he became a consulting naturalist, too. He has made studies of thirty areas in Minnesota that were to become nature centers, natural parks or camps, giving his recommendations so that people could observe wildlife with as little interference with natural processes as possible. That means that wildlife must have protected places where they can live and have their young, undisturbed by people. Humans can watch from blinds and paths and, as long as they do not intrude, wildlife will feel at home and remain.

Parks and centers open to the public in and near the Twin Cities that Les helped plan include: four Hennepin County Park Reserves, Hidden Falls and Crosby Park along the Mississippi in St. Paul, Bredeson Park in Edina and Wood Lake Nature Center in Richfield.

Wood Lake borders six-lane I-35W south of the 66th Street exit. Right next to this busy highway it is possible to cross the cattail marsh on floating boardwalks, seeing ducks, geese, muskrats, herons, shorebirds and other marsh residents at almost eye-to-eye range. Deer have found their way through the city to Wood Lake on at least three occasions. As Les says, "If the habitat is right, birds and animals will find it."

The **Anderson Lakes Park** area in Eden Prairie, south of I-494, where we lived for 23 years, is being connected by wildlife corridors with Hyland Lake Park Reserve in Bloomington and the Minnesota River Wildlife Refuge, providing summer and winter habitat for the large deer herd and other wildlife that live there. From our windows above Anderson Lake, we counted 174 different kinds of birds and many kinds of animals. One Easter morning was made very special by a rare sighting of a magnificent coyote.

Some of the most exciting moments happened when we had guests, and we were jokingly accused of staging them. Like the time we watched a hawk try three times before it caught a mouse on the ice in winter, or when a seldom-seen shrike perched on a nearby birch tree, or a pileated woodpecker came to the suet two feet from the window for the first time, and the phone rang. *No one moved.* I'll never forget the first time I saw cormorants. They were perched on dead tree stumps out in the lake, hanging their watersoaked wings out to dry after diving for fish. That was many years ago and I thought it was a very rare sight until this past spring when we saw hundreds of cormorants in western Minnesota.

In these large green spaces in and around the Twin Cities one can relax, regenerate and benefit, passively or actively, just smelling the flowers, watching the sun set through the tree tops, or bicycling, ski touring, hiking or participating in programs to learn more about the natural world we live in. Pretty terrific!

Canadian geese mate for life. The ganders are brave, dedicated and effective protectors of their partners and goslings. I once made the mistake of wading between a goose and gander while filming the goose. All of a sudden I had a back full of biting, wing-beating gander that was not willing to accept my retreat without first delivering a memorable lesson. — C.B.

Many buildings and places in the Twin Cities deserve special mention.

The State Capitol crowns one of the seven hills in St. Paul in stately fashion. Its huge marble dome, ornate carvings, and the glass star on the floor of the rotunda, symbol of the North Star State, are some of the interesting features. But my favorites are the gold horses that prance heavenward from the rooftop.

The new Science Museum of Minnesota is connected by skyway to the Arts and Science Center at 10th and Cedar. Huge prehistoric skeletons from the age of dinosaurs rub elbows with visitors who come to see the exhibits in the museum or gallery, an incredibly realistic show in the Omni Theater, a play or concert, or to attend classes. It's a busy place.

The Bell Museum of Natural History on the University of Minnesota campus, on University Avenue, has some highly prized animal and bird habitat exhibits with background paintings by Francis Lee Jaques, world renowned wildlife artist. When Les was attending the University, he would often take his bag lunch to the museum to chat with Mr. Jaques while he was working on a painting, blending the background imperceptibly with the foreground setting. Those hours led to a lifelong friendship with Lee and his wife, Florence. Before her death she donated the Jaques Gallery to the museum along with several of her late husband's paintings. Minnesota is fortunate to have this legacy of a great artist's work.

Minnesota State Capitol

Is there a more cheerful bouquet on the spring landscape than marsh marigold? Whether the day is bluebird weather or stormy, marigolds glow seemingly as bright. Large wetlands can contain *acres* of marsh marigolds, but even wholesale abundance can't detract from the specialness of these fresh beauties because they will all be gone soon, until next spring.

Golden Horse on State Capitol

The Conservatory in St. Paul's beautiful Como Park has magnificent plantings, some rare, that keep summer going all year round. When the temperature outdoors is sub-zero and the ground is white with snow, a momentary trip into a lush green world is a nice contrast.

Orchestra Hall in downtown Minneapolis, was built for the Minnesota Orchestra, one of the world's finest symphony orchestras. The acoustics are superb, but the exposed pipes and ducts in the lobby and on the exterior remind me of the ventilation system of a steamship. This is honesty in architecture, I guess, but do we have to let it all hang out?

On the outer fringe of downtown Minneapolis, across Hennepin Avenue from Loring Park, that dollop of green and blue at the end of the Mall, is **Walker Art Center**. It primarily shows avant-garde exhibits of painting and sculpture in its antiseptic galleries. We have been delighted by some and completely turned off by others, but we applaud the encouragement of creativity.

Connected to the Walker is the **Guthrie Theater**. Its thrust stage was made for the Guthrie repertory company, but many concerts, plays and operas are also performed here. I am not a true Grand Opera buff, but I do delight in the innovative renditions of operas, not all *grand*, produced by the Minnesota Opera Company.

I am particularly fond of abandoned pastures. The rich variety of plant life that carpets the land during the slow transition back to forest attracts the greatest possible diversity of animal life. From burly bears to tiny shrews, circling hawks to buzzing humming birds, voles and coyotes, foxes and grouse, snow buntings, redpolls, deer, moles, red-headed woodpeckers and bluebirds — all are drawn to, and thrive on, the old pasture. This classic grass-shrub-forest mixture is crowned by shining golden goblets — the American elm.

The more traditional home of the arts is the **Minneapolis Institute of Arts** at 24th Street and Third Avenue. It was remodeled in 1974 to house its own fine collections and visiting shows, a highly creative children's theater, and art school.

No impression of the Twin Cities would be complete without visiting the downtowns. **The Nicollet Mall** in Minneapolis is a winding tree-lined lane accented with fountains, flower beds and attractive lamplights. During the holidays the bare trees bloom with thousands of tiny lights, turning the Mall, with its festively-trimmed store windows, into a wonderland. It has become a tradition to walk the Mall on Thanksgiving night to see the decorations and lights when they are first turned on. The Mall is the heart of the shopping district where famous stores and specialty shops are centered. Branches of most of them are located in suburban shopping centers. A network of skyways makes it possible to go from one building to another avoiding both traffic and weather. The glass-walled IDS Tower is the tallest building, with an observation platform at the top. Its Crystal Court has become the hub of the downtown district.

The downtown area of St. Paul is a mixture of department stores, shops, financial and other buildings and hotels, placed without a sense of organization, but with interesting variety. The restoration of the Mears Park area provides a nice relief from modern glass and steel. In Minneapolis, similar restoration work has been done on the Butler Square building which is filled with out-of-the-ordinary shops and eateries.

Any time of the year, there is a special event to attend somewhere in Minnesota. A few pulled out of the bag are Kolacky Days in Montgomery, Stillwater's Ice Cream Social in the dead of winter, Corn on the Curb Days in Le Sueur, and Agate Days in Moose Lake. But the big events, with the most hoopla, parades, contests and queen candidates, are in the Twin Cities. The **Aquatennial** in July in Minneapolis features many water-oriented sports and a miscellany of summer activities in addition to two grand parades, balls and the final crowning of a queen chosen from all the pretty candidates. St. Paul's **Winter Carnival** events go on no matter what the weather. An ice palace is erected downtown and there is plenty of revelry in the court of King Boreas. Speed skating, snowmobile and dogsled races, ice fishing, and ski jumping are designed for the hearty who only laugh at the wind and cold.

The Minnesota State Fair, one of the largest in the nation, is a super show of the best the state has produced during the year, from art to pigs, and quilts to apples. For ten days, ending with Labor Day, the crowds come to look, eat, show their products, see a horse show in the hippodrome and attend the grandstand shows with big-name stars. I'll never forget paddling like mad at the end of a canoe trip one year so we could get to the State Fair in time to catch the Smothers Brothers show. We just made it.

Roses are red, violets are blue . . ." so the old rhyme goes, but the "Common Blue Violet" isn't blue at all, it's violet! And if I had my way, no beautiful wild thing would be called "common." That demeaning title should be reserved for the likes of house flies, *not* egrets, terns and violets! There are about forty species of violets in variations of five or more colors, depending on how color-conscious you are. Most are violet, white or yellow, but regardless of color, violets herald the welcome return of spring.

Anyone with an appetite for seeing how life was lived in Minnesota during the past century and a half, will relish touring these homes and buildings which are open to the public.

The Minnesota Historical Society Building, next door to the State Capitol, is a storehouse of Minnesota's heritage. In addition to visiting the exhibits of Minnesota's past, I recommend browsing in the well-stocked bookshop for more information on points of interest and background information on the state.

The Ramsey House, built in 1872 at 265 S. Exchange Street in St. Paul, was the elegant home of the first governor of the territory of Minnesota. Most of the original furnishings are in this fine example of the late Victorian period.

"Minnesota's most impressive remaining Italian Villa" residence, is what *A Guide To Architecture in Minnesota* calls the **Burbank Livingston-Griggs House** at 432 Summit Avenue in St. Paul. It was built during the Civil War when cost of labor was high, for $22,000! The lavish adornment and rich furnishings are reminiscent of the genteel past. A booklet published by the Minnesota Historical Society describes the house and the families that lived in it.

My first visit to the house was to attend an evening musicale. Small costumed groups were playing very old instruments in various parts of the house as we moved from one room to another. I wasn't in St. Paul that evening; I was in a fashionable Paris salon of the 19th Century.

The Gibbs Farm Home Museum at 2097 Larpenteur West, St. Paul, is a distinct contrast in architecture and living style to the Summit Avenue Burbank home. Heman Gibbs built this simple but sturdy farmhouse in 1867. His first home was a log and sod shanty built on his claim along an Indian trail in 1849. The furnishings are typical of 1860 and 1870 farm homes. A barn containing early implements, and an 1890 one-room schoolhouse are also on the property. Demonstrations are often given on Sunday afternoons of pioneer crafts such as quilting, candle and soap making. The property is owned and maintained by the Ramsey County Historical Society.

The American Swedish Institute is housed in a castle-like mansion, built in 1907 at Park Avenue and 26th Street in Minneapolis by Swan Turnblad, the owner of the largest Swedish-language paper in the U.S. It was probably built more as a showplace than a residence, since the Turnblad family lived there only briefly before moving to an apartment across the street where they could look at their chateau and live more simply. In 1929 it was given to the Swedish Institute which Turnblad founded to foster Swedish culture in this country. It is truly a showplace where one can admire the exquisite porcelain heating stoves, wood carvings, Swedish crystal, rugs and the turrets, towers and terraces.

Early morning photography excursions are constant reminders of fall duck hunts with Dad when I was a boy. The thrill of getting up in the pitch black, before there was even a hint of dawn, of quickly downing a stack of Dad's special buckwheat cakes, of feeling our way to the car with the duckboat on the trailer and gunny sacks of decoys already in and ready, of speaking in hushed voices so we wouldn't disturb those still sleeping — all are brought back.

This morning at the Carlos Avery Game Refuge would have been a good one for hunting — cool, cloudy and with the promise of a good wind to keep the birds moving. And the memory of those mid-morning snacks of jelly-filled Bismarcks is still so fresh I can taste 'em!

The Hennepin County Historical Society Museum at 2303 Third Avenue South in Minneapolis is an English Tudor mansion built in 1919 by a Minneapolis milling executive, George C. Christian, and acquired by the Historical Society in 1958. One of its most intriguing displays and collections of memorabilia is called "Main Street U.S.A." At eye level, in what was a large garage, are eleven scaled-down buildings along an imaginary Main Street, furnished with thousands of small objects typical of the turn of the century period, inhabited by charming life-like figures in delightful situations. This is our past brought to "life" with a sense of humor through many years of work by Edna Knowles King. My mother was fascinated by this exhibit, recognizing many furnishings and clothes from her girlhood.

SOUTHEAST

The highway that follows the Mississippi River south from the Twin Cities has been called one of the most scenic drives in America. "Old Man River" has carved a wide and winding path and the high bluffs on either side provide ever-changing panoramas and spectacular lookout points.

At Hastings, the first river town south of the Twin Cities, we like to browse in the antique shops. One is housed in the Le Duc Mansion, one of the finest examples of Victorian Gothic style in Minnesota, built during the Civil War.

Les and I like roaming back roads and, in the river country almost any side road winds and dips from hilltop into draws and valleys. We've learned that when following these twisting roads it's easy to lose a sense of direction on cloudy days. A compass proves very helpful.

One off-the-beaten-highway route we like is down into the Cannon River Valley to secluded Welch, nestled between sandstone cliffs, then south to Vasa and back to the Mississippi at Red Wing.

The Memorial Park Scenic Skyline Drive in Red Wing climbs to the top of Sorin's Bluff overlooking the city and the river. Below Red Wing the river widens to form 35-mile-long Lake Pepin, famous for boating and fishing.

Bluff after bluff, great ramparts confine the Mississippi River to its wild valley. Between the valley walls is an island and backwater wilderness hundreds of miles long. This broad band of wild land and water belongs to all of us for much of it is a national wildlife refuge.

One of our favorite side trips is to Frontenac State Park and Old Frontenac. The quiet settlement on the river is seemingly untouched by the 20th Century, and that's the way the residents like it. In fact, Israel Garrard, who built St. Hubert's Lodge as his home in 1856, gave land to the railroad west of town so that it wouldn't come through the village and disturb its tranquility. The Westerveldt house, built in 1854, is the oldest of several Greek Revival style homes built in the mid 19th Century. In the late 1800's many famous Americans came by river steamer to vacation, paint and hunt. Old Frontenac Inn, built in 1860, is now a Methodist Camp.

Frontenac State Park surrounds the village. There is an expansive view from the top of Point-No-Point and an Indian ceremonial rock 400 feet above Lake Pepin. During spring bird migration the park is an excellent birding place with chances to see some of the more unusual species such as blue-gray gnatcatcher, prothonotary warbler and bald eagle.

Because rivers were Minnesota's first highways, river towns were the first to be established. Lake City, whose streets are lined with many fine old homes, is located at one of the most scenic spots on Lake Pepin. An excursion boatride is a good way to enjoy some of that scenery. Water skiing began here in 1922 on a pair of homemade skis. A block-long fishing pontoon is a convenient and good place to catch over ten varieties of fish including walleyes and striped bass.

A ''nice ol' barn''

Have you ever felt very close to history? I did at this beautiful old stagecoach stop in southeastern Minnesota. I could picture the driver and guard climbing down to help passengers. This sturdy inn is a remnant of the period when stagecoach routes criss-crossed the land before the coming of railroads. Now it rests quietly beside a seldom-used country lane.

Foxtail Barley — Sunrise

November. The bright colors of fall have faded; summer birds have migrated; there's not enough snow yet for winter sports. So most folks stay home. Drab? I'd rather say that November is subdued, restrained, quiet. Empty? No, *full!* — of wildness, cleanness, brisk, invigorating air. A November day like this is one I'd unselfishly like to share with lots of kindred spirits — about a mile apart.

When my mother graduated from high school in Wabasha in 1903, it was a busy river town. A presently famous establishment was famous back then, too. The Anderson Hotel, claimed to be Minnesota's oldest operating hotel, was built in 1856, and is now operated by the fourth generation of the Anderson family. Grandma Anderson's kitchen has made the dining room a mecca for those who enjoy good food graciously served.

Wabasha is at the northern boundary of the Upper Mississippi River Wildlife and Fish Refuge which extends 300 miles south. Timbered islands, backwaters and marshes are rich in animal and plant life. One early spring day we were thrilled to see thousands of white whistling swans on the river below a wayside lookout point near Weaver.

The road to Whitewater State Park from Weaver is a paradise for those who like unspoiled wilderness. The road tunnels through dense growth, and the meandering Whitewater River comes into view every now and then.

Whitewater State Park is a Shangri-la tucked away in a valley surrounded by unusual cliffs and limestone formations. Wild turkeys, re-introduced in the area have multiplied so that a sighting of these shy birds is possible.

Winona's landmark is Sugar Loaf Bluff, rising like a sentinel high above the city. Another high vantage point, accessible by car, is Garvin Heights Park. The Steamboat museum is a sternwheeler riverboat bulging with remnants and bounty of the old boats that once churned Mississippi waters.

The drive west from Winona to Rochester is one of the loveliest in southeastern Minnesota, through rolling countryside. There is an old water-powered mill at Stockton.

Above the river road at Homer, the Bunnell House is of interest for its Gothic Revival design and details, and its historic significance. It was built about 1855 by the first permanent white residents of the county and it is now sometimes open to the public.

At La Moille we like to sidetrack over to Pickwick, a tiny crossroads center in an idyllic setting. Willows droop over the millpond reflecting a four-story mill of cut stone that still grinds feed for the farmers as it has for generations. Here time does seem to have stood still.

Wherever the state map has the word "dam" and a line across the Mississippi, there are locks through which tugboats must push a line of huge barges. We have never ceased to marvel at the maneuvering ability of the pilots who steer the barges through the locks with what seems like only inches to spare.

At Dakota we like to take County Road 12 that winds its way through a narrow canyon to the top of the bluffs, and then drive south on Apple Blossom Drive (County Road 1) to see the Mississippi Valley from topside. Near La Crescent there is a high point overlooking endless apple orchards on the slopes below, and a

Having turkey for Thanksgiving? Even though your bird may be from a farmer's all-white flock, it is a descendant of this bird's ancestors — in a roundabout way. Turkeys are native only to North and Central America. Early explorers took some turkeys, domesticated by Central American Indians, back to Europe with them. Immigrants brought them to America, and all of our modern domestic turkeys are relatives of those early travelers.

Though overshot to extinction on much of its original range, the wild turkey has been re-introduced in many states and again thrives as a game bird.

Giant Canada Geese — Rochester

I had my camera set up by this forest-bordered waterfall in downtown Pickwick (See the old Pickwick mill through the trees in the background?), when a young fisherman entered the scene. As you know, I usually exclude people from my pictures, but this boy *belongs* here, as a deer would by a wilder pool. When he saw my big view camera mounted on the tripod, he politely asked if he would be in the way if he fished the pool. I told him I was waiting for an overcast sky (clouds were building) so he could go ahead. I asked his name, expecting Chuck or Tom or Butch. "Lance Michael Henderson" was his reply. Lance lives in Pickwick and has caught many a brooky in this pool. The cast on his arm was the result of a typical kid accident. He was climbing and grabbed the wrong thing, a loose concrete block.

view into Wisconsin and Iowa as well. The road then drops down through orchard after orchard. La Crescent and apples are synonymous. Over ten varieties are grown here and shipped all over the U.S. and Canada.

Les and I have often commented on how southeastern Minnesota seems to be a treasure of scenic beauty and recreational opportunities. The Root River country offers marvellous exploration, state parks for camping and picknicking, trout streams and ponds, canoeing, swimming, golf, the usual vacation activities — and caves. Evidence of good farming practice, necessary to prevent soil erosion, is everywhere, such as wooded hillsides, contour plowing, grass runways, terracing and strip farming.

Choice Beaver Creek Valley State Park is almost hidden between heavily wooded hills with a cold, fast-moving trout stream flowing through the valley.

We like searching out old mills and there is one built in 1876 near Sheldon north of Beaver Creek Park called the Old Schech Mill.

One town name we find curious is Money Creek given to a little community north of Houston. Some say a gentleman crossing that creek that flows through town had his money tucked in his hat. The wind blew it off and his money got wet. He spread the bills on rocks to dry, but the pesky wind blew them back into the water and they floated downstream out of his reach.

Driving west from Money Creek to Rushford, we go by way of Vinegar Hill (County Road 26 and then 27). I thought I smelled vinegar the first time we traveled this road that twists around the hill, but it was just my imagination. It was named by an early settler for a hill back in Illinois. But for a drive full of nice little surprises, this can't be beat. Valleys seem to branch off in every direction as the road climbs and dips past cliff gardens and into hollows. The Vinegar Hill road is just one of dozens of side roads we've explored and loved in this region.

Although we aren't trout fishermen, we have enjoyed visiting many of the private trout rearing ponds in this section of the state. Some charge a fee for fishing, and some raise trout for restaurants, shipping the fish live. The State Fish Hatchery at Lanesboro offers some very interesting information about trout on its tours, and a chance to see some real lunkers in the brood pond.

On a hot summer day one sure way to keep cool is to visit a cave where the temperature remains at 48 degrees. Niagara Cave, south of Harmony, was discovered in 1924 by two boys looking for lost pigs. What a discovery! Today a one-hour tour leads past odd shaped formations into large chambers and onto a bridge overlooking a 60-foot waterfall with a 70-foot vaulted dome above it.

Other large caves are Minnesota Caverns and Mystery Cave southeast of Preston, with entrances two-and-a-half miles apart. Seventeen-foot-deep Turquoise Lake, a "pipe organ," "frozen" falls

Whitetail deer live virtually *everywhere* within their range — forests, brushland, cornfields, cemeteries, suburbs, even in small wild places deep within cities. It seems that if the habitat is there — browse, cover, water, enough space to outmaneuver humans and dogs, the word gets around and a few whitetails move in.

and ribbon stalactites are some of the curious features. We have been told that southeastern Minnesota is honeycombed with caves, some as yet unmapped and perhaps still undiscovered — a challenge to spelunkers. Les joined a group of these cave explorers once, and the report of straddling and jumping chasms plus crawling through narrow openings doesn't tempt me to try it.

Forestville State Park is a gem of historical interest and beauty. The original settlement of Forestville was a trading center and stagecoach stop between La Crosse and Mankato. Furs and produce were traded for flour and other supplies at Tom Meighan's store, established in 1853. Union soldiers drilled here during the Civil War. In the 1870's the railroad bypassed Forestville and the town all but disappeared. In 1910 the door was locked on the Old Meighan store of handpressed bricks and its contents. Today it's possible to browse the old store and learn a bit more of what life was like "back when." A network of park hiking trails leads to overlooks and a pioneer cemetery. Two creeks and the south fork of the Root River, known for good trout and smallmouth bass fishing, thread their way through the park.

No Minnesota city is as well known as Rochester. And probably no Minnesota city constantly gathers people from so many countries as does Rochester, all because of the Mayo Clinic, the renowned medical center founded by Dr. William W. Mayo and his sons in the late 1800's. Tours of the Mayo Clinic and Mayo Medical Museum are mind boggling. Silver Lake, within the city limits, offers a complete change of pace from the highly sophisticated Mayo medical organization. About 20,000 Canadian geese, and giant Canadian geese, once thought to be extinct, winter on the lake warmed by the power plant. Many hundreds stay during the summer, too. While the geese are tame enough to hand feed at Silver Lake, they become wild once they fly outside the city. There are few sights as thrilling as a flock of geese coming in for a landing on the water, and at Silver Lake the thrill can be repeated ad infinitum. Quarry Hill Nature Center, the Olmstead County Historical Society Museum, fine restaurants, and a wide selection of entertainment and recreational facilities make this cosmopolitan city ready for company all year round.

Around Rochester roads lead in every direction to scenic spots. One we especially like is Fugle's Mill and Museum south of Simpson. Here on the North Fork of the Root River, the mill stands as sturdy and straight as when it was built by Matthew Fugle, an immigrant from Germany. He had brought plans of his father's mill in Baden on the Rhine with him, and a dream to build one like it in America. He staked his claim here in 1854, and by 1868 had saved the $12,000 it took to build the mill. It is no longer operating, but is filled with intriguing antiques, well worth a visit.

South of Chatfield the Root River Canoe Trail begins its 74-mile flow to the Mississippi.

Did you ever watch a raccoon fish? He's mostly after crayfish, and he does it by *feel*. His little hands work back and forth through the shallows and he gets a look of intense concentration on his face. Almost like a person trying to put a very small nut on a very small bolt on the hidden back side of a bulky machine. He looks this way and that with unfocused eyes, and I almost expect him to bite a lip or stick out the tip of his tongue as he zeros in on his invisible dinner.

Scarlet Tanager

Forestville Store, Forestville State Park, is yesteryear for real. The shelves are still stocked with the quaint merchandise of grandfather's time. And there is nothing in the surrounding forest to jar you back to the present. The entire park is a lovely setting of streams, ravines and valleys, little changed by the years since the store was built of handmade bricks in 1854.

Mantorville is a charming town that has consciously preserved its 1860's appearance ever since a restoration movement inspired by Irene Pappas began a few years ago. A cut limestone hotel built in 1857, known as the Hubbell House, was a popular stagecoach stop. Today it is a fine restaurant. The stone courthouse, built in 1865, the old Opera House, newspaper office, the Congregational church, the "Grand Old Mansion" of the Stussy family, and the old Episcopal church, now the Dodge County Historical Museum, are all accent pieces in this town where almost every home and building fits the restoration theme. Let's hope more towns follow Mantorville's example before precious landmarks disappear.

Compared with the time when it was larger than Rochester, the community of Wasioja, northwest of Mantorville, is almost a ghost town. Once on a territorial stagecoach route, it boasted a fairground, race track, limestone slab sidewalks and a newspaper. When the railroad bypassed the town, all these disappeared, but some landmarks remain. The old stage hotel is now a home. The Baptist church is believed to be the oldest of its denomination in the state. A huge rock in the yard of the stone schoolhouse wore out plenty of pants and shoes when used as a slide. At the southeast edge of town, almost hidden in a spruce grove, stands the lonely skeleton of Wasioja Seminary. When recruits for the Civil War were called for, ninety of the students marched to the stone Recruiting Station (built for a bank and still there) to enlist. That closed the school. It burned in 1905 leaving its stark remains.

SOUTH CENTRAL

Mention Northfield and Jesse James comes to mind. James, the notorious bank bandit, raided the Northfield bank in 1876. But Northfield also is a peaceful college town on the Cannon River with two beautiful campuses. At St. Olaf, the highlight of the year is the Christmas concert season. Tickets are hard to come by but we were lucky to be guests of friends one year to hear the famous choirs and orchestra following a sumptuous smorgasbord at the college which included my first taste of lutefisk, that famous Scandinavian delicacy. At Carleton College, on the other side of town, the May Fete is an annual event.

If time allows, we take the scenic route between Northfield and Faribault via Nerstrand Woods State Park. Here is a remnant of the "Big Woods" of oak and maple that once stretched from the Mississippi River to Mankato, sheltering Indian villages and pioneer settlements.

Faribault was founded by Alexander Faribault whose frame house built in 1853 still stands at 12 N.E. First Avenue. Bishop Whipple, who was a nationally-recognized champion and friend of the Indians in the mid 1800's, established three well-known schools in Faribault: Shattuck Military Academy, St. Mary's Hall and St. James School for Boys. The Peony Farm in June, Crysanthemum Gardens in September, great caves for curing blue cheese, and the Faribo Woolen Mills are some of the attractions that draw thousands of visitors to Faribault.

Before the coming of agriculture, southern Minnesota was covered with a rich mixture of forest and prairie. Both gave way to the plow to help feed a hungry world. Today, remnants of either prairie or forest are treasured as rare bits of natural beauty, and many are preserved in state parks, The Nature Conservancy holdings, or as nature centers. This lovely stream flows through the Jay C. Hormel Nature Center at Austin.

SOUTHWEST

The southwestern section of Minnesota isn't usually considered tourist country, but Les and I have found travel here very interesting. There are numerous reminders of dramatic events that shaped pioneer life in Minnesota, many of them from the summer of 1862 when the Dakota (Sioux) Indians waged an all-out war to drive the white man from the Minnesota River Valley.

With history so recent one can almost hear the thunder of buffalo hooves as they stampede into oblivion and the haunting echo of Indian drums. Prosperous farms and modern cities now cover the land, but searching out visual evidence of our past adds a special purpose to a trip through this lush green countryside dotted with blue lakes.

It has been almost beyond our comprehension as we have stood in quiet, secluded Traverse des Sioux State Park, two miles north of St. Peter, to imagine 8,000 Dakota (Sioux) gathered on this site. They had come in July, 1851, setting up tipis in tiers around a central treaty ground, to negotiate with representatives of the U.S. Government. Here thirty-five chiefs signed away nearly 24 million acres in Iowa and Minnesota for 12½ cents an acre. (The same treaty was signed at Mendota on Pilot Knob two weeks later.) Within a few months the land boom was on, and white settlers rushed in to establish farms and villages along the length of the Minnesota River.

Dissatisfaction over terms of the treaty, delays in payment and promised food were some of the reasons given for the Sioux Uprising eleven years later.

Minneopa Falls in the State Park at Mankato is almost a sister to Minnehaha Falls in appearance, tumbling into a deep, rocky and wooded gorge. An interesting old stone windmill in the park has been restored. Prairie flowers abound in the area adjacent to the campgrounds. Les and I once spent a beautiful morning there photographing blazing stars in full bloom.

The scene at Mankato's Sibley Park, where the Blue Earth and Minnesota Rivers meet, was quite different in 1701. The previous fall Pierre Le Sueur and a crew of Frenchmen struggled up the Mississippi in two canoes and a sailboat to this point, expecting to find a bonanza in copper ore. After building the valley's first fort, and consuming 400 buffalo during the winter, they dug 30,000 pounds of earth, and Le Sueur took 4,000 pounds of the best "copper ore" back to France, only to learn the blue clay was worthless.

One year, Les and I made a special trip to Jeffers Petroglyphs as a way to celebrate my birthday. Hearing about the rock carvings done by hunting peoples as long as 5,000 years ago, I *had* to see them. We drove the county road west from Comfrey and turned south on County Road 2 for a mile to the entrance. What appears to be a rather low, treeless ridge holds secrets of the past yet to be revealed.

The spring flowers of the woodlands may be but distant memories in August, but cone flowers, blazing stars, asters and countless other prairie splendors are at their peak — *right now!* This prairie in Big Stone National Wildlife Refuge near Ortonville, is one of the few remaining in Minnesota. — C.B.

Minneopa Falls State Park — Mankato

I could almost hear the thundering hoofs, the falsetto whoops of the Sioux as they drove the bison herd toward the lip of the cliff above me. But no buffalo have been chased over this cliff at Blue Mounds since the white man broke the sod of the surrounding fertile prairies. Bison are up there today, but braves no longer haze them. A token herd again grazes the good grass, supervised by the Blue Mounds State Park staff. This is a good place to look at Minnesota history. It seems very close.

No one knows for sure who the people were who pecked at the red rock outcroppings, leaving crude but recognizable pictures of bison, bear, wolf, turtle and elk, and human stick figures, some holding atlatls, a spear-throwing device used to increase the power of the human arm. Many other glyphs added to our feeling of awe.

On the north side of the Minnesota River between Fort Ridgely and New Ulm is the old Harkin-Massopust general store returned to its 1870's appearance by the Minnesota Historical Society. Les and I met the granddaughter of the original owner several years ago when she graciously showed us the curious items left in the store at the time it closed in 1901.

New Ulm has lots of personality, history and oompa-pa. Its broad streets and beautiful parks were planned in every detail by Christian Prignitz, one of the German immigrants who settled here in 1855. The city has retained and nourished its German heritage, evident in the architecture of the old postoffice, two organizations, The Turnverein for physical fitness and the New Ulm Battery, a civilian military unit, and two picturesque breweries; special events such as the Polka Festival when the streets bounce with happy rhythms of its many dance bands; and Herrmann, who stands with his sword raised high, cast in bronze on the hill above the city. Les teases me about Herrmann who is one of my heroes, but I consider him worthy of veneration. Herrmann was a great German warrior who led his tribes in battle to end the oppressive rule of the Romans over

Prairie — Minnesota River Valley

Beyond the white darkness . . . ? Yesterday there were farms in the distance below this prairie bluff at Blue Mounds State Park. But this morning the wild prairie continues to the invisible horizon at the edge of the world. Bison bulls rumble their statements of invincibility back over the hill to the left. (They really do. There is a herd here grazing on the prairie grasses.) So maybe when the fog lifts, a circle of tipis will be a Sioux campground below. At least until the air is clear enough to discern them once again as farm buildings.

his people 2,000 years ago. Herrmann Lodges of the U.S. erected this huge monument in his memory. A climb up the stairs of the monument gives a great view of the city.

New Ulm suffered heavy losses in the Sioux Uprising of 1862 when almost two hundred buildings were destroyed. Three that survived can be seen today: The Dacotah Hotel at 111 N. Minnesota Street, which served as a hospital; the Erd Building, now a restaurant at 108 N. Minnesota Street, where settlers took refuge in the basement with a keg of powder intending to destroy themselves if the Indians took the settlement; and the Forster Building, 117 N. Broadway, where bullet holes are still visible on the north wall. The Brown County Historical Society Museum at Broadway and First Street North has more information about the Uprising.

Monuments commemorating events of the Uprising are scattered throughout southwestern Minnesota, testimony to lives lost in that bitter conflict.

Fort Snelling was never attacked, but Fort Ridgely, now a state park on the upper Minnesota River, was the scene of two of the fiercest battles of the Sioux Uprising. Walking over the ground of the Fort today, the story of bravery and heroism on both sides unfolds in dramatic fashion.

On August 20, 1862, four hundred Indians attacked, and two days later an estimated eight hundred Indians attacked the Fort manned by 180 poorly armed men. The Fort, built in 1853 to protect white

Minnesota Farm

Snow-melt and spring rains provide a steady, slow flow of ankle-deep water through this black ash swamp. These are obviously ideal conditions for marsh marigolds, resulting in this grand display for about one week each spring. One feels there should be a festival to honor such a magnificent event! But there was no one else here as I picked my way in hip boots, trying to avoid crushing the showy blossoms. I tilted the lens forward on my 4 × 5 view camera to hold the entire field of flowers in sharp focus.

settlers, was merely a group of buildings without a stockade, vulnerable from three ravines. Three hundred settlers had streamed into the Fort on August 18 and 19 for safety, complicating its defense. If the Indians had attacked then, they would have found only a handful of soldiers led by a 19-year-old lieutenant who had the mumps. Captain Marsh, the post commander had left on the 18th with a company of forty soldiers to aid the settlers at the Lower Sioux Agency who had been attacked that morning. He lost his life with twenty-four of his men when ambushed by the Sioux at the Redwood Ferry.

By the time of the first attack on Fort Ridgely on the 20th, the Fort's defense had increased from twenty-nine to almost 180 men. A well-drilled crew, manning the post's few cannons, is credited with driving off the Indians.

Today the stone commissary has been rebuilt and the log powder magazine restored. Archeological excavations have uncovered foundations of other buildings, and artifacts reveal much about the Fort and its occupants.

The Lower Sioux Agency, southeast of Morton on County Road 2, was built in 1853 as an administration center for the first Dakota (Sioux) reservation, established by the treaties of Traverse des Sioux and Mendota. It resembled a small village with stores, shops, mills, dozens of homes and a stone warehouse. Eight years of pressure by the government, traders and white settlers on the Dakota climaxed in their rebellion.

At sunrise on August 18, 1862, Dakota warriors staged a surprise attack, killing twenty white people and burning and looting the buildings. Upper Sioux Agency buildings were also sacked and burned. Battles at New Ulm, Fort Ridgely, Birch Coulee and Acton followed before the Indians were finally defeated at Wood Lake. On September 26, 269 white and mixed bloods captured by Dakota were freed at Camp Release near present day Montevideo. Nearly 2,000 Dakota were tried in the weeks that followed, and 307 were sentenced to death. President Lincoln lowered the number, and thirty-eight were hanged at Mankato on December 26, a sad moment in a sorry period of American history.

An Interpretive Center at the Lower Agency has exhibits depicting the history of the Eastern Dakota Indians from 1800 to the present.

Parks, bluffs and gorges make Redwood Falls an especially beautiful city. Steamboats once unloaded supplies on the Minnesota River, and the cargo was carried from here by oxcart to North Dakota. The town had a gold rush in 1894, but after a year of digging up buckets of shiny quartz, the prospectors left and the promoters disappeared. But a real "gold mine" started in 1886. An enterprising young depot agent named Dick Sears notified other agents that he had unclaimed watches for sale. The "mail orders" netted him $500, and that was the birth of Sears Roebuck and Company. Redwood Falls still encourages ingenuity, hosting an Inventors' Congress each year in June.

Whitetail fawns are about as lovable as an animal can be. But they all have mothers and should be left untouched! Not only is it illegal to take a fawn home, it is dangerous. Hand-raised deer grow quickly, and without fear of humans, they are a problem. If loose, they are apt to be shot. And even though adult deer are beautiful and a delight to have around, the sharp-hoofed, sharp-antlered animals can, in an instant of frustration, do severe damage to people or other pets.

One gentleman who pops up repeatedly in the stories of early events in Minnesota is Joseph R. Brown, another of my "heroes." I wish we could have known him for he seems to have been in on the beginning of things when men of action and foresight were needed. Starting as a drummer boy at Fort Snelling in 1819 while the fort was being built, he went on to be a soldier, fur trader, lumberman, founder of cities, legislator, editor, Indian agent and inventor. Sinclair Lewis once said, "Perhaps as much as anyone, he was the inventor of the automobile."

He brought his wife, Susan, of French, Scottish and Sioux blood, and their twelve children to live in a nineteen-room granite mansion on a slope overlooking the Minnesota River beyond the white settlements. Elegantly furnished (two grand pianos, crystal chandeliers and damask drapes), it was the center of hospitality in the late 1850's. In 1862, while Mr. Brown was in New York to see about his inventions, the Sioux Uprising broke out and his wife and children were captured and the home was burned. Because Mrs. Brown could speak the Indians' language, she and the children were held captive but unharmed until their release at the end of the Uprising. Remnants of the walls and a plaque showing how the original house probably looked are located on County Road 9 south of Sacred Heart.

In the Granite Falls vicinity along Highway 212, is some of the oldest rock on the crust of the earth, probably 3.7 billion years old, close in age to our planet itself. It was exposed by the erosive action of the ancient River Warren which flowed from melting glaciers 10,000 years ago and by highway construction.

During spring and fall migration periods, serious birders and people who merely enjoy the sight of birds, gather at well-used flyways. This past spring, Les and I joined a group of birders in the Salt Lake area near the South Dakota border to welcome flocks of cormorants, white pelicans, geese and smaller birds as they arrived from the South. It's a dead heart that doesn't quicken its beat at seeing skeins of geese shifting positions as they come closer, calling to each other in muted tones, then circling and dropping in on a Minnesota lake for the first time that year. What a marvelous phenomenon, migration.

On a night walk we heard snipes, their tail feathers whistling in aerial courting flights, and owls hooting in the woods.

The Lac Qui Parle, Marsh and Big Stone Lake Reservoirs are all great birding and scenic areas. The western grebe, famous for its curious mating rituals and spectacular dancing, and the short-eared owl can sometimes be seen here. Potholes in the prairie are good places to see shorebirds not common in other parts of Minnesota such as the Wilson's phalarope that spins like a top in the water to stir up its prey, avocet, little blue heron, yellow-crowned night heron, and snowy and cattle egret.

Across the Minnesota River from Lac Qui Parle State Park is an intriguing historic site. Joseph Renville, son of a French fur trader and Sioux mother, was an expedition guide for Pike in 1805, then a captain on the British side in the War of 1812, before coming here to trade with the Indians about 1822. With servants and bodyguards he lived "in splendor quite like an African king" with his Indian wife. Renville invited missionaries to establish a Protestant mission and often participated in services himself. Here missionaries began translation of the Bible into the Dakota (Sioux) language and Indians were taught agriculture and weaving of cloth. A replica of the mission chapel on the original site is a museum of Indian artifacts and pioneer relics.

One year, we timed a visit to Pipestone National Monument to coincide with a performance of "The Song of Hiawatha" pageant. It is given on the last two weekends of July and the first one in August at the edge of the monument. Sitting in the natural ampitheatre, watching the legend made famous by Longfellow come alive on the shore of Lake Winona was a beautiful and memorable experience.

The Pipestone Quarry is one of the best known American Indian sites. For centuries Indians have come here to get the red stone for their ceremonial pipes and figures. Many legends relate to the area and the stone, some romanticized and some authentic, but there is no doubt that the pipe was smoked in sacred rituals by many tribes. Few white people knew of the quarry until the noted artist of Indian life, George Catlin, came from New York in 1836 to sketch and to secure samples of the stone. In his honor the pipestone was named catlinite. Two years later the U.S. government sponsored an

exploring expedition of five men led by Joseph Nicollet. Their carved initials can be seen on Inscription Rock. In his report Nicollet mentioned three huge boulders called the Three Maidens. He told of Indians placing offerings in front of them before digging at the quarry.

A self-guiding circle trail goes by part of the quarry. Les and I watched in fascination one evening as an Indian aimed his blows at just the right places to split huge chunks of the red rock. Only Indians are allowed to quarry the stone.

There are many points of interest along the trail such as Leaping Rock, a stone column twenty-three feet high, separated from surrounding ledges. Leaping to this rock and not losing one's balance was considered a feat to boast about. John C. Fremont, a member of Nicollet's 1838 expedition, successfully made this leap.

The trail winds up and down along lichen-covered rock cliffs, past delicate Winnewissa Falls and out onto the prairie. Just the variety of plantlife and flowers makes walking the trails an adventure.

The museum has exhibits on the quarry and its legends, and pipestone items made by the Indians are for sale.

South of Pipestone, near Blue Mounds State Park, lives one of my favorite authors, Frederick Manfred. Some of his novels are based on Indian legends or stories of early frontier life such as *Lord Grizzly* and *Conquering Horse*; others seem to grow from the soil of his beloved "Siouxland." *Scarlet Plume* is a tale of the Sioux Uprising in southwestern Minnesota.

NORTH CENTRAL

Stick a pin anywhere in the map of northern Minnesota and you'll probably hit a forest, a lake with good fishing spots and swimming beaches, a golf course, resort, summer cabin or campground, or a town or city that caters to vacationers. This is the promised land for thousands of folks who are drawn northward by sparkling lakes and rivers and opportunities to relax and enjoy the great outdoors.

This is the land of the legendary logger, Paul Bunyan, where forests of giant pines were cut and floated down rivers to lumber mills. The days of the big log drives are over, but the memory of Paul is kept alive in Brainerd and Bemidji, where giant statues of him are almost "life size." We have seen his girlfriend at Hackensack and his "birthplace" at Akeley. All the lakes are allegedly hoof prints of Babe, his Blue Ox. Thanks to Babe, but more likely the glaciers that once covered Minnesota, there are some whoppers, like Mille Lacs, Leech, Cass, Upper and Lower Red, Winnibigoshish, Rainy and Lake of the Woods. In between are literally thousands more of lesser size but no less beautiful.

A taste of what real logging camp life was like can be sampled at the Rapid River Logging Camp north of Park Rapids where meals are served in the Cook Shanty lumberjack style. Tom's Logging

Camp and Museum on the North Shore of Lake Superior beyond Duluth is a reconstructed camp with boardwalks connecting the bunk house, blacksmith shop and mess hall, all filled with tools and furnishings of pre-chainsaw days.

It would be unfair to emphasize one area more than another for vacation facilities, but information isn't hard to come by. Information centers in almost every town are happy to tell visitors about accommodations and special events. Some special places and activities shouldn't go unmentioned, however. They are like accents in the music of the northland which can be anything from a sweeping wilderness symphony to a rollicking country polka.

Itasca is the Queen Mother of Minnesota's state parks, established in 1891 to preserve the true head (verITAS CAput) of the Mississippi as determined in 1832 by the research of Henry Schoolcraft who was guided by an Indian.

Many outstanding specimens of our state tree, the red (Norway) pine, are in the park, especially in Preachers' Grove. The largest red pine in Minnesota is in the park just off the Wilderness Road. It is 120 feet tall and over 300 years old, an awesome patriarch. Nearby, at Nicollet Creek, is the bison site, the oldest archeological site in

People come, as if on a pilgrimage, to step across the small stream flowing around boulders from Lake Itasca. They take pictures of each other balancing precariously on the slippery rocks to put in the family album as a reminder of this historic moment. For this is the source of the Mississippi River which flows from this point over 2,300 miles to the Gulf of Mexico.

An estimated million visitors come to Itasca State Park each year, not only to walk across the Mississippi, but to enjoy the magnificent forest of towering red and white pines, to hike the trails, observe and learn about wildlife, fish, camp, picnic, dine at Douglas Lodge, or just "get away" from the routine of life back home.

the state. Excavations of bones of an extinct bison, much larger than today's buffalo, and artifacts indicate that nomadic hunters ambushed bison as they forded the stream 7,000 to 8,000 years ago.

When in Itasca State Park it's interesting to note some facts about Minnesota and its watersheds, indicated by those wavery rather thick gray lines on the state map. Minnesota is located approximately in the center of the North American continent. The state slopes from the north central portion near Itasca in four directions. Minnesota's supply of water, unequalled by any other state (one square mile of water for every 20 of land) flows south down the Mississippi River, north to Hudson Bay, east to the St. Lawrence River through the Great Lakes, and southwest to the Missouri River. At a point between Hibbing and Chisholm is a three-way divide. From that point, water flows to the Arctic, the Atlantic and the Gulf.

On Lake Itasca or almost any other northern Minnesota Lake, there is a sound that captures attention — a weird lonely cry, or a wild laughing call. These are the unmistakable calls of the common loon, Minnesota's state bird.

The streamlined loon, which is much larger (8 to 12 pounds) than a duck (1 to 3½ lbs.), is sleek black and white with a necklace of vertical black and white stripes and ruby red eyes. Because of its

weight, it has to run on the water, splashing for some distance before it's airborne. On its sunset flights above the treetops, its tremulous call can be heard a long way. The loon is awkward on land but a superb diver and swimmer, pursuing fish at great depths. Observing them dive and guessing where they will pop up again can be great fun. These symbols of our wilderness are protected by law and should never be molested.

A nice change of pace on a vacation is the chance to freshen up after a day of fishing, tennis or golf, and see a play. Summer theaters present popular titles near Bemidji, Brainerd, Alexandria and in Duluth and Fergus Falls. In Grand Rapids plays are staged on a showboat.

Near Brainerd is a replica of an 1870 village called Lumbertown, U.S.A. Many old buildings and furnishings have been moved to the site, and a stroll down the boardwalks provides some amusing as well as informative moments. The drone of Brainerd car races can be heard throughout the summer, drawing thousands of spectators. Like most other vacation centers in the lake regions, there are many choices of things to do. There is an Aquarium at Park Rapids, paper

Cloudy days are *not* dull days during the fall color season. Sugar and red maples, oaks, aspens, birches and shrubs all seem to glow with an inner light on sunless days. The absolute silence of this October morn seemed so right that I found myself holding my breath as I listened to the quiet.

mills to tour in cities such as Grand Rapids, art fairs and galleries, and museums such as the ones in Bemidji and Walker.

On May 22, 1927, news flashed around the world that Charles A. Lindbergh, Jr. had successfully flown solo nonstop from New York to Paris, and the world had a hero. Everywhere wild, joyous celebrations greeted the modest, unassuming young flier whose boyhood home was Little Falls, and Minnesota promptly claimed him as "her son." Shortly after his historic flight, what seemed like everyone in Minneapolis and St. Paul, including my family, mobbed the old airport landing field to catch a glimpse of "Lucky Lindy" and his plane, "The Spirit of St. Louis." I remember my usually dignified mother frantically pulling me through the crowd so we could get a better look before he was whisked away in a limousine.

Young Charles spent winters in Washington, where his father was a Minnesota congressman, and summers at "the farm." The house, now the focal point of Lindbergh State Park, has been restored and furnished to look as it did from 1907 to 1920. A duck pond that Charles built in 1919 has his name scratched in the concrete. When we walked down to the nearby stream, one of his favorite haunts, a beautiful brown mink "flowed" over and between the rocks in a leisurely departure. The Interpretive Center on the bank of the Mississippi River has exhibits that tell of three generations of Lindberghs, including the very distinguished career of Charles, Jr., after his famous flight.

Outside the urban centers there are thrilling sights that can often be the highlight of a vacation. They aren't scheduled and there's no guarantee you'll see them, that's what makes the sight of any animal in the wild a special event. Even though Les and I have spent many years camping and observing wildlife, the excitement of watching *any* animal or bird, large or small, has never worn off. But I've discovered the bigger the animal, the harder my heart pounds.

The monarch of our wilderness is the moose, who likes to feed on tender branches and leaves of trees and bushes and on swamp vegetation above and under the water. We were surprised once to see a calm pond explode when a moose surfaced from feeding on pond lily roots. It's hard to comprehend how large a moose is until you get too close for comfort. They stand six to seven feet at the shoulder and weigh up to 1500 pounds. The male has a "bell" hanging from his neck and grows a pair of broad antlers each year. These are covered with a velvety skin until fall when he polishes them off, ready to fight for a cow. We might consider the cow moose ungainly, with her hump back and huge nose, but a bull is willing to risk his life in battle for her. During most of the year, moose will

Free again of its winter casing of ice and snow, a northern stream sings a happy song of spring. A late snowstorm could again drape the forest in a foot-deep blanket, but the stream will remain open and any set-back will be brief.

Bloodroots — Early Sign of Spring

When I look at this lovely northern stream I think of wolves! Why? Because while camping nearby the night before, in anticipation of taking this picture, I heard timber wolves sing three times. With each chorus I leaped from my sleeping bag and stood in the frigid air listening intently, for I was hearing some of the rarest, most exciting music in the world.

avoid human confrontation but in autumn the male may charge unexpectedly at anything that disturbs him — even railroad locomotives.

The graceful white-tailed deer is Minnesota's other antlered animal, red and sleek in its summer coat, gray in its winter coat of hollow insulating hairs. We think this is the most beautiful North American animal and our spines still tingle when we spot one, or a group, nibbling in a field near the edge of a woods as we slowly drive down a country road just before sunset. Chances of seeing any wildlife are usually best from a car, as animals are accustomed to them. The sight or scent of a moving person can send them leaping or scurrying for cover.

When I'm apprehensive about meeting up with a bear in the woods, Les keeps telling me I'd be lucky to ever see a bear. That statement would usually be true in the winter when bears are hibernating, but I don't know how "lucky" campers feel when a prowling black bear makes off with their food supply. I'll have to admit it's true, though, that other than the bears who have learned that certain campsites are free cafeterias, they will avoid contact with humans and run away.

Another denizen of the deep woods that is rarely ever seen but is sometimes heard "singing" is the timber wolf. He is the much maligned and misunderstood "villain" we heard about in childhood fairy tales, and the image is hard to change. Recent studies have shown what a remarkable, intelligent animal the wolf is, living in a very structured, well regulated society. But he has a bad fault — he likes to eat meat, just as most people do, and there lies the eternal conflict. Northern Minnesota is the last place where wolves live in any appreciable numbers in the lower 48 states.

For many people vacationing in northern Minnesota, the most spectacular and memorable sight is a display of Aurora Borealis or Northern Lights. There is no describing the wonder of these shifting colorful patterns of light that leap and dance in the night sky in absolute silence.

Built to be functional, but oh, how beautiful! Made from materials of the surrounding forest, log cabins and snowshoes were pioneer necessities. Today both still do their thing very well and give some of us a nostalgic closer tie to our Earth and to our past.

Immature Black-crowned Night Heron

I find the constant flow of water reassuring. Shorelines rise and fall during wet and dry years, but I doubt that the flow of canoe country rivers has stopped completely since the glaciers melted. In times of drought, if we can hold out long enough, it *will* rain again.

Our canoe "The Voyageur"

Few foods can tickle the taste buds so delightfully as the wild foods of Minnesota. Wild rice, growing in shallow lakes, has been a staple food of the Indians for centuries. To harvest it they carefully tap the ripe kernels into their canoes as they pole through rice beds. When Les was a boy, wild rice was breakfast cereal at their house. Now it's a gourmet treat found in the supermarket with a high price tag, but well worth it for special occasions. Wild blueberries, strawberries and raspberries, free for the picking, are far more flavorful than domestic varieties. Finding yourself in a good patch of wild berries can be sheer ecstacy. For sportsmen, Minnesota has long been a happy hunting ground for deer, grouse, pheasant and waterfowl. Fish, fresh from a cold-water lake and into the frying pan, is something to write home about. And something to *take* home as a gift or to savor with your own pancakes on winter mornings, is pure maple syrup from a Minnesota sugar bush.

There are many flowers that are more colorful and showy than blueberry blossoms, but few promise taste treats to equal wild blueberry pie!

Wild Roses

It's one of those magical mornings following an ice storm, when all the woods have been transformed into a shining filigree of crystal. Even the solid black trunks have been encapsuled in ice and are cold and smooth to the touch. The woods are clean, fresh, and filled with music — the tinkling, chiming notes made as the wind fractures the ice in the treetops. — C.B.

The Mille Lacs Indian Museum, operated by the Minnesota Historical Society on the west shore of Lake Mille Lacs, is an excellent place to see how the Dakota (Sioux) and Chippewa Indians lived, to learn about the decisive and dramatic battle that drove the last Dakota tribe from this area, and the effect of the fur trade on both tribes. Life-size dwellings in settings of the four seasons, and many artifacts, tools and furnishings, show how the Indian was able to live with and from nature.

Maple sugar products and handcrafted items of birch bark and buckskin, made by the Chippewa Indians of the area are for sale, and tribal dances are performed on Sunday afternoon at the Indian Community Center near the Museum.

Excavations in Mille Lacs-Kathio State Park have unearthed copper scrapers and knives made by prehistoric Indians who lived at Petaga Point between 3,000 and 1,000 B.C. Other excavations have shown significant habitation by other cultures. An interpretive Center on Petaga Point focuses on the fascinating archeology of the area.

On the bank of the Snake River just west of Pine City, is the reconstruction of a North West Company fur trading post. Documents and archeological excavation revealed just how and where the fortified post was built. One log building 18 × 77 feet divided into several rooms was surrounded by a stockade. After only one winter's use, 500 beaver skins plus muskrat, deer and bear skins, wild rice and maple sugar obtained in trade from the Chippewa Indians, were taken to the Fond du Lac collecting post on Lake Superior for eventual shipment to Europe.

The reconstructed post authentically duplicates the construction methods, crude furnishings, equipment and the simple life of the original post. We were offered some left over beans still simmering on the open fire by one of the voyageur crew who spoke with an exaggerated French accent — maybe not an authentic French accent, but a colorful one.

October's bright blue weather is really something! Some years Indian summer doesn't even happen, or it could be only one day, or five, or as much as two weeks or more. But when it does, every day is a bonus! Soft, soft air, frosty nights and pleasant days when the temperature could go into the seventies. But even on warm days one is comfortable in wools because the humidity is low. This, by far, is my favorite season. Enjoy it, my friend, tomorrow the ground could be white!

Rural Winter Landscape

As I was walking a woodland path near our home, a movement near the ground caught my eye. I knelt down to see what was moving the vegetation, and discovered that some of the leaf movement was not leaves at all, but this just-emerged luna moth. From its cocoon on the ground, the moth was climbing to a stem with enough clearance to spread its great wings for the first time.

Thinking it would rest there, I memorized the spot and dashed to the house for a view camera and tripod. Still there. I kept an eye on the moth while I uncased and set up, then composed the picture under a black cloth. The lens was just inches from the lovely moth, but the shock of emergence was still its primary concern, so it posed quietly while I took its picture.

NORTHWEST

A section of Minnesota as well known for prosperous farms as for vacation lakes lies to the west and northwest of the Twin Cities. This is not the northwoods; forests are apt to be of oak, basswood and maple rather than pine, spruce and balsam. But the lakes are just as great for fishing, swimming and boating; most are rimmed with year round or summer homes and resorts. One year we filmed a fishing movie called "A Bass in the Hand," and got well acquainted with the lakes in this region which produce crappies, sunnies, bass, walleyes and northerns big enough to please any fisherman.

Some of the special events in this section include rodeos and horse shows, steam threshing bees, fishing contests, golf tournaments and summer theater plays. Potholes and fields make for excellent duck and pheasant hunting. Two scenic lookout points are Inspiration Peak, a state wayside park west of Parkers Prairie, and Mt. Tom in Sibley State Park north of Willmar. Indians once burned singal fires on Mt. Tom which is the highest point in fifty miles. We remember the town of New London, nearby, as one of the most charming in the state. The Federal Fish Hatchery there stocks lakes of the region.

Sauk Centre is the birthplace of Sinclair Lewis, who made the town famous as the assumed setting of *Main Street*, the novel that shocked small towns across America. His boyhood home at 812 Sinclair Lewis Avenue (formerly Third St.) has been restored to its early 1900's appearance, and the Sinclair Lewis Museum is in the public library. Lewis won international acclaim as the first American to be awarded the Nobel Prize for literature. Before he died in 1951 he had written twenty-three novels including *Babbitt, Elmer Gantry* and *Arrowsmith*.

A 200-pound stone tablet found in 1898 near Kensington tells in runic carving of an exploration journey in 1362 by 8 Swedes and 22 Norwegians. Some scholars have called it a fake while others have defended its authenticity. The stone itself may or may not be a true record of an early expedition, but there is other evidence we have seen that leads me to believe that at some time Norsemen explored this land. "Mooring stones" such as the one in the park at Hawley have been found along a waterway from Lake Winnipeg in Canada to Sauk Centre. They are similar to ones found in Massachusetts and Delaware and along lakes and fjords in Norway and Sweden. In each large stone a triangular shaped hole slants downward toward the lake so a ring bolt or pin would be held securely for mooring a sizable boat. When we were in Hawley we learned that one of these stones was found at the site of the Kensington Runestone and a stone at Cormorant Lake was looked for and found because of the message on the Runestone. A Viking sword, firesteels, axes and spearheads have been unearthed, mostly by accident, all adding to the intriguing mystery. Wouldn't it be great if someday the hull of a Viking ship was found on a lake bottom! That would be the key piece to the puzzle. Meanwhile, Alexandria, proclaiming itself the "birthplace of America," guards the runestone and other artifacts in its museum, and displays a giant replica of it in a highway park. A statue of the "world's tallest Viking" stands in the heart of town.

In 1931 a repair crew working Highway 59 north of Pelican Rapids, uncovered the skeleton of a girl about fifteen years of age. It is considered to be America's oldest human skeleton, possibly 10,000 years old. The skeleton, dubbed *Minnesota Man*, with a clamshell pendant and elkhorn tool found with her are owned by the University of Minnesota. A highway marker stands at the site of discovery on the lakebed of ancient Glacial Lake Pelican.

Northwest of rolling, lake-studded hills and lively, thriving cities, the land suddenly flattens out. This is the Red River Valley, part of the lakebed of prehistoric Glacial Lake Agassiz which at one time was 100 to 600 feet deep and larger than all of the Great Lakes combined. Upper and Lower Red Lakes and Lake of the Woods are remnants of this ancient lake. Buffalo River State Park is located on Campbell Beach, one of the known beaches that formed as the water of Lake Agassiz receded. The Glacial River Warren flowed south from the lake, cutting through the continental divide at Lake Traverse and carving out the broad Minnesota River Valley.

The black topsoil in the old lakebed is deep and some of the most fertile in the world. Farms are large here. Fields of sugar beets, potatoes, wheat, barley, oats, sunflowers, soybeans and onions stretch to the horizon across the level landscape. My first reaction at seeing such flat land was almost the same as when I first saw mountains. They are both vast and awesome. Mountains can almost overpower with their height; here the land seems endless, topped with a huge, open sky. There is no interference other than farm buildings visible from miles away.

At the Old Crossing Treaty Site, west of Red Lake Falls, bands of Chippewa Indians ceded almost ten million acres of fertile land in northwestern Minnesota and northeastern North Dakota to the U.S. Government in 1863. The treaty site was on the Red River Oxcart Trail, one of the state's first important roads. Caravans of creaking two-wheeled carts drawn by oxen transported furs and other goods from Red River settlements to St. Paul, and carried supplies from the city on the return trip. A huge cottonwood tree in the park was used as a "post office," where messages were left to be picked up or delivered by those passing by.

We were just lucky to be at Old Mill State Park northeast of Warren on the one day of the year when the steam-powered mill is fired up to grind grain for neighboring farmers. They stood patiently in line with their bags of grain, because "you can't get better flour anywhere else." The friendly camaraderie made it seem like one big family reunion. We experienced that same friendly spirit everywhere, though. Maybe that's the mark of a Minnesotan — friendly.

Rural home, Moose Lake, Minnesota

EAST

Now that we live near Moose Lake, between the Twin Cities and Duluth, we like to vary the routes we take on trips back and forth. What we consider one of the most beautiful and interesting drives in Minnesota follows the St. Croix River. The St. Croix was the first Minnesota river to be preserved under the National Wild and Scenic Rivers Act of 1968. The purpose is to preserve streams having "outstandingly remarkable scenic, recreational, geologic, fish and wildlife, historic, cultural, or other similar values," for present and future generations. The St. Croix in its various sections lives up to all these requirements and it was one of the original eight rivers in the nation to be approved under the act.

The old river towns have a mellowed quaintness that makes them more precious as years go by.

Taylors Falls has a wealth of interesting old homes. The Folsom residence up the hill on Government Street, built in 1853 has been

Look. Look hard. The day after tomorrow these maple branches could be bare. Would I hold them if I could? No! It's the fleeting beauty that makes fall days so precious.

Church in Marine-on-St. Croix

restored by the Minnesota Historical Society and is open to the public on certain days. The public library, with its fringe of gingerbread, was originally a tailor shop where Civil War uniforms were made.

One of the most popular attractions in Minnesota for a day's outing is the famous Dalles of the St. Croix in Taylors Falls. This is a fantastic area of potholes created in prehistoric times when swirling waters of the Glacial St. Croix River rotated boulders and pebbles in gigantic whirlpools, grinding away the volcanic rock. Glacier Kettle, one of eighty potholes, is sixty feet deep and twelve feet across. From launch rides on the St. Croix River, some of the bizarre formations in the rock cliffs are visible, such as the 80-foot tall "Devil's Chair." Canoes can be rented, too, with pick-up service for a do-it-yourself river trip.

Few towns in Minnesota can match the quiet, undisturbed charm of Marine-on-St. Croix. An early sawmill town, it is desirable today as a lovely off-the-beaten-path place to live.

One of the nicest things to happen between two states is the St. Croix River. Very wild upstream, the St. Croix is unspoiled, with few exceptions, all the way to its union with the Mississippi. And wonder of wonders, with few people and little industry along its banks and bluffs, the St. Croix is perhaps the cleanest river of its size in the country excepting Alaska.

In 1848 the future state of Minnesota was born at Stillwater. My hero, Joseph R. Brown, one of Minnesota's most energetic pioneers, headed a delegation to establish the Territory of Minnesota. Henry Sibley, the state's future first governor, was sent to Washington to speak for them.

Lumbering was the Territory's first great industry. Until 1914 logs floated down rivers to the St. Croix "Boom Site" northeast of town. There they were sorted by the owner's mark stamped on the ends of the logs and rafted to sawmills. Today a canoe trip on the St. Croix in the fall is a never-to-be-forgotten experience, gliding downstream from Taylors Falls or O'Brien State Park to Stillwater on a sparkling carpet of blue between walls of brilliant reds and golds. Canoe rental and pick-up service are available at all three points. "Pocket Parks" with sandy beaches on wooded islands make ideal picnic spots.

Lowell Inn, one of the nation's most famous hotels and restaurants, known as the Mt. Vernon of the West, dispenses hospitality and fine food in a gracious setting. As thousands of other newlyweds have done, we spent our wedding night at Lowell Inn.

An intriguing self-guiding tour of historic homes in Stillwater leads up the steep hills for glimpses of the exterior of homes built in the heyday of lumbering. Some fascinating examples are "Grandma Bean's Playhouse," a parody on architectural styles; a house overlooking the river with a watchtower and siding resembling stone; one labeled "carpenter's frenzy," and others with Italian, Moorish, Greek, Federal and Victorian influence. The Washington County courthouse, one of Minnesota's oldest and most beautiful, stands on a lofty site at Pine and Third. Recognized for its historic and architectural importance, it is preserved as a historic site.

Minnesota's first bridge — Stillwater

There are few secrets in the winter woods. Until the next snow, the comings and goings of forest creatures are easily read.

Knowing about the past, about the land, who the people were who first came and what they did, can add to your enjoyment while traveling through Minnesota.

This book is not meant to be a travel guide, but it points out some places that Les and I have found to be of special interest through our own experiences. In this brief account, many places are omitted, but that leaves exploring and discovery for you to do, and that's a good part of the fun. Get off the highways. Do a little research ahead of time. And enjoy!

If I'm away from Minnesota during the fall color season, I feel as if I've skipped a part of my life. So when I'm here, I try to be at all of the best places at once. That's difficult when it takes all day to drive about twenty miles, stopping every quarter mile to saturate my eyes, as well as film, with delicious color. This birch and maple forest is in the Tamarac National Wildlife Refuge.

SUGGESTED INFORMATION SOURCES ON MINNESOTA:

Minnesota Official Highway Map

Minnesota Tourist Information, Dept. of Economic Development, 480 Cedar, St. Paul, Minnesota

Minnesota, A History, by William E. Lass. Pub. by W. W. Norton & Company, New York

Minnesota: A History of the State, by Theodore C. Blegen, revised edition. University of Minnesota Press

The Story of Minnesota, by Jerry Fearing. Pub. by the Minnesota Historical Society

Minnesota's Major Historic Sites, Second Edition, by June Holmquist and Jean Brookins. Pub. by the Minnesota Historical Society

The Streams and Rivers of Minnesota, by Thomas F. Waters. Pub. by the University of Minnesota Press

Minnesota's Rocks and Waters, by Schwartz and Thiel. Pub. by the University of Minnesota Press

Meet My Psychiatrist, by Les Blacklock. Published by Voyageur Press

Ain't Nature Grand!, by Les Blacklock. Published by Voyageur Press

Minnesota Seasons (Calendars) by Les and Craig Blacklock. Published by Voyageur Press

Minnesota Birds: Where, When and How Many? by Janet Green and Bob Janssen. Pub. by the University of Minnesota Press

A Birders Guide to Minnesota, by Kim Eckert. Distributed by the Minnesota Ornithologists Union, James Ford Bell Museum of Natural History, University of Minnesota, Minneapolis

A Gathering of Waters (Canoe Routes in Minnesota) Minnesota Dept. of Natural Resources

Field Guides to Birds, Flowers, Butterflies, Ferns, Insects and other subjects are available in book stores

The Voyageur, reprint edition, by Grace Lee Nute. Minnesota Historical Society

The Sioux Uprising of 1862, by Kenneth Carley, second edition. Minnesota Historical Society

The Doctors Mayo, by Helen Clapesattle. University of Minnesota Press

The St. Croix, Midwest Border River, by James T. Dunn. Holt Rinehart Winston

Tigers of Como Zoo, by Edythe Records Warner. Published by Voyageur Press

Tall Timber, by Tom Bacig and Fred Thompson. Published by Voyageur Press

Sinclair Lewis — Home at Last, by John Klobas. Published by Voyageur Press

Chippewa Dawn, by Don Spavin. Published by Voyageur Press

Fort St. Charles, by Sister Noemi Weygant. Published by Voyageur Press

Grazing, Minnesota Wild Eater's Foodbook, by Mike Link. Published by Voyageur Press

Minnesota in Books for Young Readers, by Grace Swenson. Published by Voyageur Press

Postcards of Early Minneapolis/St. Paul. Voyageur Press

Postcards of Early Duluth. Voyageur Press